Corner House Publishers

SOCIAL SCIENCE REPRINTS

General Editor MAURICE FILLER

OF SIX MEDIÆVAL WOMEN

WITH

A NOTE ON MEDIÆVAL GARDENS

POET DECLAIMING TO ACCOMPANIMENT OF VIOL.

Frontispiece.

OF SIX
MEDIÆVAL WOMEN

TO WHICH IS ADDED

A NOTE ON
MEDIÆVAL GARDENS

BY

ALICE KEMP-WELCH

WITH INTRODUCTION AND ILLUSTRATIONS

CORNER HOUSE PUBLISHERS
WILLIAMSTOWN, MASSACHUSETTS 01267
1972

FIRST PUBLISHED 1913

REPRINTED 1972

BY

CORNER HOUSE PUBLISHERS

Printed in the United States of America

AUTHOR'S NOTE

THE Author's acknowledgments are due to the Editor of *The Nineteenth Century and After* for his kind permission to reprint such of the following studies as have already appeared in that Review, and also to "George Fleming" (Miss Constance Fletcher) for her rendering, on page 146, of four verses of Christine de Pisan's poem on Joan of Arc.

CONTENTS

ILLUSTRATIONS

OF SIX MEDIÆVAL WOMEN

INTRODUCTION

THE recent researches of scholars and students have brought the study of mediæval times within the range of almost any one who cares to live in imagination in the past. No part of this study has been more advanced and made more informing to us than that which regards the individual. This is specially true of womankind, of whom we have learnt somewhat, in some instances from their own writings, and in others from allusions to their work in those of contemporary and later writers, and also, incidentally, from the vast storehouse of didactic literature, which is so suggestive in itself, reflecting through successive centuries, as it seems to do, the standard of conduct of the large majority. But on this subject—a very large one, and only partially explored—light can only be thrown gradually. For this there are various reasons. One is that, until comparatively recent times, the small details of everyday life which go so largely to make up a woman's life, have generally been taken for granted by writers. Then the few mediæval historiographers and chroniclers were principally engaged in recounting the deeds of kings and feats of arms. Then again, although probably many MSS. of the time still lie undiscovered in libraries, those that are known to us are scattered far and wide. Furthermore, self-advertisement was not a mediæval fashion. It is perhaps difficult for us nowadays to understand a spirit of self-effacement. Self-esteem, which may develop for either good or ill, has perhaps always existed in the human breast, but certainly since the time of the Renaissance, when it seemed to have its own special revival, it has grown apace, and is to-day like unto the Mustard Tree of Holy Writ. But it is not proposed to contrast this our modern attitude with the impersonal one, if so it may be called, of the Middle Ages, because, whilst there were many humble, zealous workers then, just as there are now, it is possible there were other and perhaps more potent factors to account for this apparently humble attitude. In mediæval days, the subject of a narrative or didactic work was considered so important, that an author would scarcely venture on any independent treatment of a theme for fear of incurring censure for a contempt of authority, or, if he did so venture, he would probably deem it wiser to do so anonymously, or by ascription to some departed celebrity, who was obviously not in a position to gainsay him. The writer was of much less interest than his ideas and sentiments. Then again there was the intense localisation of life. Localities were very independent of one another. Each was complete in itself, and within it there was no need for self-advertisement. It was the same in the wider life of associated religious communities, such as Benedictines, Cluniacs, and Cistercians, who had so much to do with the building of abbeys and cathedrals. Within a fraternity, the specially gifted craftsman was known, and wherever work was going on within the Order, was made use of as needs be, not as Brother This, or Brother That, but simply as scribe, or as artificer in Madonnas or gargoyles, or whatever else was wanted. The glorification of the community as a whole, and not the advertisement of the individual, was the desired goal. This self-effacement was not so much humility, though of course that too existed, as the special form which communal feeling took at that time. Now if this suppression of the individual was true of men, how much more true must it have been of women, who seldom ventured beyond town, or castle, or convent walls. In truth, women hardly appear on the scene, and English women least of all. It is only women who were prominent through their high official positions, either political or religious, such as Blanche of Castile, or St. Catherine of Siena, or the Abbess Hildegarde, or women like the Blessed Angela of Foligno,[1] or Julian, anchoress of Norwich,[2] or some other of the devout women of mediæval Italy, who interpreted the mysteries of divine love to mediæval society, having in fact, as it were, religious salons, from whom the veil has been withdrawn, and even amongst such as these it has sometimes been only very slightly lifted. With these saintly and political women must be mentioned the women doctors of Salerno—Trothula, Abella, Mercurialis, and others—who played so important a part both as professors and practitioners when this school of medicine was at its zenith in the eleventh and twelfth centuries, and who left behind them, as evidence of their learning, treatises which are of interest to-day as showing mediæval methods in medicine.

Still, even so, the records are scanty. In order, therefore, to form some idea and estimate of women generally in the Middle Ages, we must perforce fall back on reasoning from the

[1] *The Book of the Divine Consolation of the Blessed Angela of Foligno.* The New Mediæval Library.

[2] *Revelations of Divine Love recorded by Julian, Anchoress of Norwich, 1373.*

known to the unknown, and, by studying the few who are recorded in written history, judge of that great majority who, though nameless, have yet so largely helped to make up the world's unwritten history. Just as many a flower blooms and dies unseen, so many a woman must have lived her life, serviceable to her special environment, but wholly unrecorded. Just as, in the course of ages, the seeds of some humble plant have been carried by wind or water from some lonely region to one less remote, and made to serve a purpose by adding to the sum-total of beauty and usefulness, so the thoughts and deeds of many an unremembered woman have doubtless passed into the great ocean of thought, encircling us to-day, and influencing us as a living force.

Thus we have the women who figure in history, and whom we must take as types of the influential woman of the time, and the women whom history has not so honoured. Of the former, even when only portrayed in outline, we can learn something, but how are we to learn anything of the latter, whether living in the seclusion of religious houses or in the world? Of those living in religious houses, we know from records that, besides attending to their own spiritual and mental education and tending the sick, they conducted the cloister schools and taught in them needlework, the art of confectionery, surgery, writing, and drawing. They also wove, and embroidered, and added their mite to the sum-total of beauty by transcribing and illuminating MSS. of the Gospels and of the lives of the Saints. But sometimes such a limited sphere of activity was enlarged, and it is to an anonymous Anglo-Saxon nun of the eighth century, to whom the experiences were related, that we owe one of the earliest and most interesting accounts extant in Northern Europe of a journey to Palestine.

To learn something of those living in the world, who were the inspirers, the helpmates, and the companions of men in everyday life, we must turn to the poems and romances. These form the key to the domestic life of the time. Though ordinary life may be somewhat idealised in them, still it is ordinary life on which they are based. Moreover, many of the MSS. in which they are written down contain miniatures —a legacy of exceeding worth to the student. But if we seek some knowledge of mediæval life from miniatures, it is not necessary to confine our researches to MSS. of romances. Transcripts of the classics, of the moralised Bible, and of other religious works also supply many pictures of everyday life, adapted quite regardless of incongruity, for one of the characteristics of the Middle Ages was a profound incapacity to picture to itself anything *but* itself, or to reconstitute in any way, as we do to-day, times and scenes not its own. This was owing partly to its vitality and its youthfulness, which grasped at anything and everything without discernment, and partly to its lack of reliable material. The whole aspect of life, too, was changed and enlarged, and for the moment over-charged, for the flood-gates of the East, hitherto only partially opened, had been rent asunder by the traveller and the crusader.

Before we attempt to arrive at some idea of the manner of life of the women of the Middle Ages, it will be well, if possible, to modify what seems to be a general and perhaps a distorted impression of these women of bygone days, as regards their want of loyalty in their domestic relations, and all the deceit and cunning such a want led to. Without attempting to justify what is fundamentally wrong, let us go if we can into the region of fact, and in that region there is quite enough romance without introducing it from outside.

In the first place, so much more, as a rule, is heard of vice than of virtue. "La voix de la beauté parle bas : elle ne s'insinue que dans les âmes les plus éveillées." Then the standard of life in those days was very different from what it is to-day. Manners and customs which were

accepted facts of everyday life then, would strike
us as strangely rude and repellent now. Take,
for instance, the attitude towards his queen of a
king we have all been taught to revere—Arthur,
the semi‑saint, and the so‑called pattern of
courtesy. When Guinevere deserts him, and
some of his knights are slain, his remark—not
whispered into the ear of a confidant, but uttered
aloud in the presence of all around him—is, " I
am sorrier for my good knights' loss than for the
loss of my fair Queen, for queens I might have
enow." Such a sentiment, expressed in public,
does not seem quite up to our modern standard
of courteous, or even civilised, conduct, and yet
here we have the sentiments of the Prince of
Chivalry, as conceived by the poets of the
thirteenth century. So it is obvious that before
passing judgment upon the standard of life of
the mediæval woman, we must endeavour to
arrive at the truth by thinking and living in
imagination on the same plane, as near as may
be, as she did.

Then again, it is largely owing to certain
stories in the Middle Ages that the women of
those times have been defamed. If we consider
the sources and the transcribers of these stories,
we shall perhaps find a reason for their distorted
outlines, filled in with so much imperfectly
understood detail. Many of these tales originated

in the East, and particularly in India, where the conditions of domestic life led to and favoured intrigue, and many of them also were mere allegory, in which the Eastern sought to hide great truths. These the less meditative Western interpreted literally, mistaking the outward form for that which it concealed. So in passing to the West, Eastern ideas and Eastern exaggeration, misconstrued, became caricature. Moreover, the compilers of these stories were often monks or minstrels who vied with each other for popular favour, the monk introducing into his legends material which he hoped would rival the often shameless out-pourings of the minstrel, whilst the minstrel, for his part, tried to adorn his story with some moral. Naturally neither class of such purveyors was in the least capable of judging woman with respect, or indeed of judging woman at all.

On the other hand, however, it must be remembered that there are stories that tell a very different tale, a tale of self-sacrifice and devotion in face of grievous trial, as, for instance, that of Eric and Enide, sung by Chrétien of Troyes, and made familiar to us by Tennyson's poem of " Geraint and Enid." It is impossible that such a conception should have been the mere outcome of the poet's imagination, since a poet, whilst he may transform, focuses and reflects the ideas of his time. In truth, we find mediæval literature, if we try to estimate it reasonably, gives a quite pleasing impression of womankind, whether we turn to some of the royal ladies who presided over brilliant Courts, where learning was encouraged and poets made welcome, or to the lady of lesser degree, who reigned supreme in her castle, at any rate when her lord was away, as was often the case in time of war or during attendance at Court, or to the abbesses who governed the religious houses they were set over, to their material and mental well-being, proving thus their genius for administration, and, in many instances, their rare intellectual attainments. A record in a chartulary of the Benedictine nunnery of Wherwell in Hampshire, now in the British Museum (Egerton MS., 2104), and accessible to all in translation in the second volume of the *Victoria History of the County of Hampshire*, may be mentioned in passing, since it gives such a charming picture of mediæval convent life. It recounts the life and work of the Abbess Euphemia, who presided over the house from 1226 to 1257. Amongst her many good deeds, it is told of her that " with maternal piety and careful forethought, she built, for the use of both sick and sound, a new and large infirmary away from the main buildings," and that, besides caring thus for the bodily wants of her community, "she built there a place set apart for the refreshment of the soul, namely a chapel of the Blessed Virgin." The writer adds that "in numberless ways she provided for the worship of God and the welfare of the sisters," and that "she so conducted herself with regard to exterior affairs, that she seemed to have the spirit of a man rather than of a woman." The account is altogether delightful and informing, and should be read by any who would go in spirit to a mediæval convent. It is therefore not surprising that in the late Middle Ages a regard and reverence for womanhood gradually arose—a regard and reverence for woman not merely as the weaker vessel, but as the principle of all good and of moral elevation. This attitude was also in large measure due to the inevitable fusion of the cult of the Virgin and the cult of woman, which in the thirteenth century developed into a faith. Then was it that religion and chivalry, in combination, formed the solvent that disintegrated the layer of selfishness—the outcome of the worship of brute force—that had settled over. man's nobler instincts, and by their appeal to his better nature decided the position that woman, not only as an individual, but also as a class, was thenceforth to take in the civilised world.

Let us now turn, first to the woman of the

Romances and then to the woman of History.
Each completes and is completed by the other.
For the woman of the Middle Ages there were
practically only two alternatives—to enter into
the bonds either of Holy Matrimony or of Holy
Church.   In both cases the vows were, as a rule,
taken early, especially in the case of marriage, so
that the woman of the Middle Ages knew little
of the joys of girlhood, with all its romantic
castle - building and fondly fostered illusions.
From playing with dolls, the child of twelve
or even younger often suddenly found herself
transformed into a wife.   Although the Church
had decreed that no girl should be wedded
before the age of fifteen, this mandate was often
ignored in noble families, where, through death,
large fiefs had been left without a male representative and protector.   In such a case the
over-lord considered it necessary to assert his
authority, and compel the marriage of some
young girl of perhaps only twelve, so as to
secure for her vassals and retainers a qualified
leader, and for himself the needful and pledged
military service.   Still these marriages of con-
venience were often really happy arrangements,
for the girl-wife had been trained to altruism,
and its principles were the very essence of her
daily life.   Love, moreover, is a subtle sprite,
and just as surely as he can spread his wings and

fly away, so he can come, as if at unconscious bidding, and make for himself a dwelling-place.

To get any true insight into the life of the woman of the Middle Ages, we must study the small everyday affairs, and to this end go, in imagination, to some castle, and see how the day is passed there by its lady. Perhaps it is a day in late spring. The watchman on the tower, heralding the day, has sounded his horn, and soon all the castle is astir. Leaving her curtained bed, she first offers a short prayer at the small shrine hanging close by with its flickering light. Then the bath, the water scented with aromatic roots and covered with rose-petals, is taken. Mass and the morning broth follow, and the day is considered fitly begun. The poor, or any sick and sorry folk, are the first to be considered, or perhaps there is some wounded knight, who has sought shelter within the protecting walls of the castle, for whom soothing potions or healing salves have to be compounded. This latter service was generally the work of the lady of the castle, who as a rule possessed sufficient surgical knowledge to bind a broken limb. To beguile the weary hours of convalescence, she sings to the lute, tells stories, recounts legends, or reads aloud a romance lately bought from some wayfaring packman. Little is it to be wondered at that the convalescence is protracted, or that the knight delays his departure from day to day, sometimes to his own and the lady's undoing.

Beside such varied ministrations, the woman of the Middle Ages rode to the chase, went out hawking, snared birds with nets, ferreted rabbits, spun, wove, and embroidered. Embroidering was a really formidable occupation, for the great hall, and each room, had its special hangings, and on fête-days every inch of wall-space was covered. One set would picture an Arthurian legend, and others again were made bright with flowers, lilies, roses, and columbines. The lady and her maidens—often girls of noble birth, whom it was customary to send to some castle to complete their education—worked at the countless yards such decoration involved, and chatted the while, it may be, of some coming marriage or tourney, or perchance one among them would tell a story, and so time passed merrily enough. Then for the educated woman, of whom there were many, Latin verse offered a wide field of delight, and the woman of the Middle Ages read and loved her Virgil just as we of to-day read and love our Shakespeare. When the daylight had faded, there was always chess-playing, dancing the carole, and singing, and by the thirteenth century little pastoral ballets, in which a knight, and a shepherdess and her lover, took part, began to be produced for the diversion of castle-folk. For daily entertainment, every castle of any pretension had its own minstrel or minstrels, whilst in the smaller castles a wandering singer was warmly welcomed. Sometimes the lady gave audience to a poet, who read his latest idyll, a minstrel, to the accompaniment of his viol, singing the interspersed lyrics. Such a scene may be found depicted in miniatures, and suggests how such a story as " Aucassin and Nicolette," and many another, partly in prose, partly in verse, was rendered. One such miniature shows a lady reclining on a couch, with a lordling seated beside her, the poet, with his small parchment leaflets, declaiming his story, the minstrel waiting to take up the theme in song. It is of interest to note that in this particular miniature the gown of the lady is ornamented with heraldic devices. By such means we are enabled not only to identify the person represented—since portraiture, even if there was anything worthy of the name, was in a very rudimentary condition— and thus arrive at the approximate date of the picture, but also to verify a custom, and a stage in social life. It was not until the end of the twelfth century, when some sort of heraldic system became necessary owing to the introduction of the closed helmet, that armorial bearings,

hitherto mere personal badges, became attached
to noble families.　By the thirteenth century,
when the bourgeoisie had become rich, they
were worn by the sumptuously attired wife of
the lord to distinguish her from the equally
sumptuously attired wife of the wealthy burgher.

Such, in mere outline, was the daily life of
the mediæval lady. Descriptions of the lady
herself seem to be mere replicas of an admired
and fixed type, for there is in them such a same-
ness of delineation, that we can only imagine
that poets sang of qualities that pleased, and did
not attempt to individualise. All are good and
gracious, beautiful, and slight of figure, with
delicate hands and tapering fingers, small feet,
fine and glossy hair, and grey eyes, laughing and
bright. Only occasionally are these attractions
varied and enhanced by the telling of beauty
unaided by paint and hair dye.

It is hardly necessary to speak, save very
generally, of woman's dress, for much has already
been written on the subject. For everyday use,
garments of wool or linen, according to the
season, and with much fur in winter, were worn.
At weddings or tournaments, or on any other kind
of fête-day, the ladies vied with each other in
rich cloth of gold and silver, in silks woven with
threads of gold and patterned with conventional
design, and in all kinds of iridescent silken stuffs

from the East. From Mosul, on the banks of the Tigris, whence the material we call muslin takes its name, was brought a fine silk gossamer, something like our *crêpe de Chine*. This was used for the finely plaited underdress seen at the neck and foot of mediæval costume. Perhaps the best representation of this, although stone seems hardly the most favourable medium for the delineation of so delicate a fabric, can be seen in the long slim figures of the queenly ladies standing in the niches on either side of the west door of Chartres Cathedral.

But when we have contemplated this gorgeous and dainty apparel, and all the other personal luxury that accompanied it, such as enamelled and jewelled gold circlets for the head, jewelled girdles with each jewel chosen for its own special virtue, carved ivory combs, tablets and hand-mirrors, and the like, we are forced to wonder how all this refinement and beauty could go hand in hand with so much that is unpleasing. If we turn to consider the manners of the men, we find the same contrasts—on the one hand the maximum of gallantry and courtesy, and on the other a corresponding churlishness and brutality. Metaphorically and actually, the lance and the battle-axe were still rivalling each other in the warfare of daily life. Although the battle-axe must eventually yield to the lance, still strange extremes have flourished side by side all down the ages. Turning to but comparatively recent times, the coarseness we associate with much of the reign of Charles II. stands out in glaring contrast with the delicate, graceful poetry that found expression then. And coming still nearer to our own days, we think of the unseemly manners in the reigns of George III. and IV. and the dainty miniatures such as those painted by Cosway, and wonder how these could exist together. Might we not just as well wonder why the olive tree has a gnarled, distorted stem, whilst its delicate, symmetrical leaves, of the tenderest green grey, glisten in the sunshine like silvery shells fresh from ocean's bed ?

Renan, amongst the many thinkers on life's mysteries, tells us that " Life is the result of a conflict between contrary forces." But to philosophise is useless, and it is still more useless to question life's seeming anomalies. We can only bow in silence before " what Time in mists confounds."

As has been already said, it is only a general idea of the women of the Middle Ages that can be gleaned from the Romances. For something to bring us into more real touch with them, and to reveal more of their personality, we must consider some who have made themselves known to us through their work, since history, until we come to the fourteenth century, is almost silent about them. Thus it is that as we study these women, it almost seems at first as if we were looking at some faded frescoes in a dimly lighted church. But just as the half-obliterated figures take form and life as our eyes grow accustomed to the dimness, and our minds get attuned to the days that knew their living representatives, so these women of whom we are speaking may live again for us if only we treat their works as human documents, and not as archæological curiosities. The following pages tell of six such women who lived between the tenth century and the first half of the fifteenth—Roswitha, a nun of Germany ; Marie de France, a lady at the Court of Henry the Second of England ; Mechthild of Magdeburg, mystic and beguine ; Mahaut, Countess of Artois, a great-niece of St. Louis ; Christine de Pisan, an Italian by birth, living at the Court of Charles the Fifth of France ; and Agnes Sorel, the Mistress and inspirer of Charles the Seventh.

In trying to evoke the women of these days of long ago, it is hardly possible to do more than portray them in outline. Yet even so, if the outline be true, we may remember, for our consolation, that it has been said that we shall never, except in outline, see the mysterious Goddess Truth.

ROSWITHA PRESENTING HER POEM TO THE EMPEROR OTHO I.,
THE ABBESS OF GANDERSHEIM STANDING AT HER SIDE.

A. Dürer, 1501.

To face page 1.

A TENTH-CENTURY DRAMATIST, ROSWITHA THE NUN

In this age of personal curiosity, politely called psychological interest, when personalities are analysed with all the thoroughness of the dissecting theatre, it seems almost courting failure to try to call to remembrance one whose personality has long since faded away, and of whom, apparently, no contemporary writer has made mention. Of Roswitha, the woman, we know but little, and this little is gathered from her own writings.[1] Presumably the date of her birth was about A.D. 935, and that of her death about A.D. 973. There is a tradition that she was connected with the royal house of Germany, at that time represented by the enlightened Otho the Great. Be this as it may, her life for us begins when, probably at an early age, she entered the Convent of Gandersheim. Gandersheim was a Benedictine nunnery in the Harz Mountains, founded in the ninth century by Liudolf, Duke of Saxony, and important enough

[1] The authenticity of these has been called in question by some critics, but apparently upon insufficient data.

to entitle its Abbess to a seat in the Imperial
Diet, a right perhaps never exercised except by
proxy. The story of its foundation, as told by
Roswitha in the unique MS. of her works, is
of strange beauty. Listen to her own words as
she tells the tale :—

At that time there was, nigh unto the Monastery,[1] a little
wood, encircled by shady hills, those same hills by the which
we ourselves are surrounded. And there was, moreover, in the
wood a small farm where the swineherds of Liudolf were wont
to dwell, and within the enclosure of which the men, during
the hours of night, composed to rest their weary bodies until
the time when they must needs drive forth to pasture the pigs
committed to their care. Here, on a time, two days before
the Feast of All Saints, these same herdsmen, in the darkness
of the night, saw full many bright lights glowing in the wood.
And they were astonished at the sight, and marvelled what
could be the purport of this strange vision of blazing light
cleaving the darkness of the night with its wondrous brilliance.
And all trembling with fear, they related unto their Master
that which they had seen, showing unto him the place which
had been illumined by the light. And he, desiring by very
sight thereof to put to proof that which he had heard tell,
joined them without the building, and began the following
night, without sleeping, to keep watch, closing not his eyes
though they were weighed down by the desire of slumber.
And after a while he saw the kindling lights, more in number
than afore, once again burn with a red glow, in the same place
forsooth, but at an hour somewhat earlier. And this glad
sign of happy omen he made known so soon as Phœbus shed
his first rays from the sky, and the joyous news spread everywhere. And this could not be kept back from the worthy
Duke Liudolf, but swifter than speech did it come to his
ears. And he, carefully observing on the hallowed eve of the
approaching festival whether perchance some further like
heavenly vision would clearly show it to be an omen, with
much company kept watch on the wood all the night long.

---

[1] The first foundation, afterwards removed to Gandersheim.

And straightway when black night had covered the land with darkness, everywhere throughout the wooded valley in the which the very noble temple was destined to be built, many lights were perceived, the which, with the shining splendour of their exceeding brightness, cleft asunder the shades of the wood and the darkness of the night alike. And thereupon, standing up and rendering praise to God, they all with one accord declared it meet that the place should be sanctified to the worship of Him who had filled it with the light. And, moreover, the Duke, mindful of his duty to Heaven, and with the consent of his dear consort Oda, forthwith ordered the trees to be felled and the brushwood cut away, and the valley to be completely cleared. And this sylvan spot, aforetime the home of fauns and monsters, he thus cleared and made fitting for the glory of God. And then, before obtaining the money needful for the work, he at once set out the lines of a noble church as traced by the splendour of the red light.[1]

In suchwise was the building of our second Monastery to the glory of God begun. But stone suitable for the structure could not be found in those parts, and thus the completion of the sanctuary which had been begun, suffered delay. But the Abbess Hathumoda, trusting to obtain all things from the Lord by faith, oft-times, by serving God both night and day with holy zeal, wore herself out with too abundant labour. And with many of those placed under her care, she besought the solace of speedy help from Heaven, lest the work so well begun should be left unfinished. And of a sudden she became aware that the divine grace which she sought was present, ready to have compassion on her longings. For as she lay one day prostrate nigh unto the altar, fasting and giving herself up to prayer, she was bidden of a gentle voice to go forth and follow a bird she would see sitting on the summit of a certain great rock. And she, embracing the command with ready mind, went forth, putting her trust in it with all her heart. And taking with her very skilled masons, she sped swiftly whither the kindly Spirit led her, until she was come to the noble sanctuary which had been begun. And there she saw, seated on the lofty summit of the self-same rock, a white dove,

---

[1] For other instances of churches laid out on lines said to have been revealed in dreams or visions, see Didron, *Christian Iconography*, vol. i. (1886) pp. 381, 382, 460, and Sta. Maria Maggiore, Rome.

the which, flying with outspread wings, straightway went before her, tempering its flight in unwonted way so that the virgin, walking with her companions, might be able to follow in a straight course its aerial track. And when the dove in its flight had come to the place which we now know was not wanting in great stones, it descended, and with its beak pierced through the ground,[1] where, beneath the soil, many stones were disclosed. And assured by this sight, the very worthy virgin of Christ bade her companions clear away the heavy mass of earth, and lay the spot bare. And this done, supernal and devout piety presiding over the work, a great wealth of mighty stones was brought to view, whence all the needful material for the walls of the monastery already begun, and of the church, could be obtained. Then, striving ever more and more with all their heart, the builders of the temple destined to be consecrated to the glory of God, laboured at the work by night and by day.

Thus does Roswitha tell how the work of the new Foundation was begun, the Duke Liudolf and his wife having already journeyed to Rome to ask of the Pope his blessing, as well as to beg of him, as a token of his favour, some sacred relics to deposit there. The Pope, giving them his blessing, thus makes answer to their request :—

There were here, aforetime, two mighty rulers—the most holy Anastasius who presided over this See, and his co-apostle, the holy Innocent. These, through their services to the Church, were the most famous next after St. Peter and

---

[1] The intervention of a bird to aid in discovery was a favourite tradition derived from antiquity. We may recall, amongst many variants of the theme, the story of the celebrated expedition of the Athenians to the Island of Scyros to find and recover the body of Theseus. Theseus, being a hero, the agent employed in the quest must likewise be distinguished, and so the eagle, Zeus's bird, is alone thought worthy to peck the earth and indicate the resting-place of the demi-god.

St. Paul. With such care have the illustrious bodies of these two been heretofore preserved by all the rulers of this city, that never has any one been permitted to carry away the least portion of them, and thus their sacred limbs remain undiminished. But forasmuch as it is meet that I yield to your pious request, I will grant you, without recompense, tokens from both these sacred bodies, cut before your very eyes from off the sacred bodies themselves, if so be that you will make solemn oath to me to venerate these relics in your community, of the which you have made mention, preserving them for all time within your Church, sacred hymns being there sung by night and by day, and a light being alway kept burning. And of our apostolic right we ordain, according to your request, that your community be of our See, to the end that it may be secured from all secular rule.

And Liudolf, with glad heart, made promise of this, and returned home with the coveted relics.

The MS., now at Munich, which tells this fascinating story of love and faith, was, it is considered, written about A.D. 1000, and was fortunately preserved in the Benedictine convent of St. Emmeran, Ratisbon, where the scholar and poet, Conrad Celtes, discovered it at the end of the fifteenth century. It also includes metrical legends, a fragment of a panegyric on the Emperor Otho, and six dramas. Of such worth were these latter counted, that when Celtes published the MS. in 1501, Albert Dürer received a commission for an ornamental title-page, and for a frontispiece to each of the plays. It is by these dramas that Roswitha has distinguished herself in the world of letters; for although the legends contain points of interest, and are treated with skill, they are naturally not so unique as the dramas, nor do they reflect her personality in the same way. She herself tells us that the plays were written in imitation of the manner, but not of the matter, of Terence, and that her only desire in writing them was "to make the small talent given her by Heaven to create, under the hammer of devotion, a faint sound to the praise of God."

But before considering her work, let us glance at her own life, and the life of contemporary Saxon nunneries.

Nearly one hundred and fifty years before the supposed date of Roswitha's birth, the hitherto untamed and warlike Saxons had been finally defeated by the mercenaries of Charlemagne, and, as one of the signs of submission, forced to embrace Christianity. But having submitted, they forthwith, and with an aptitude suggestive of the spirit of the modern Japanese, set themselves to appropriate, assimilate, and remodel for their own use, the rudiments of the civilisation with which they found themselves brought into contact. So speedy and so thorough was the transformation, that scarce a century passed ere the once powerful Frankish kingdom of Charlemagne bowed down before the strenuous Saxons, to whom the supreme power was transferred. Their Chief was elected king of the Germans, and some fifty years later their king, Otho the Great, after being crowned at Aix-la-Chapelle, the former centre of Frankish rule, received the Imperial Crown from the Pope in

COVER OF ST. EMMERAN GOSPELS.

Tenth Century.

To face page 7.

MARRIAGE OF OTHO II. AND THEOPHANO.

Byzantine, 10th century.

To face page 7.

Rome. This displacement of the political centre was naturally followed by a complete displacement of artistic centres. Both these sides of life were fostered by Otho with a keen personal interest—the building up of his empire and the encouragement of art going hand in hand. Moreover, owing to his close ties with Italy and the East, and the element of classic tradition inevitably induced by such ties, art received an added stimulus and grace. Oriental monks were to be found in the monasteries. Learned men and artists were summoned from Italy and Constantinople. The number and influence of these were increased when Otho's son, afterwards Otho the Second, married Theophano, a Greek princess, who, bringing many compatriots in her train, sought to reflect in her German home something of the learning and splendour of the Byzantine Court. The ivory, shown in illustration, commemorating this marriage, is an example of the work of some Byzantine craftsman in her employ, whilst the jewelled and gold-wrought cover of the Gospels of St. Emmeran (now at Munich) shows to how high a level the goldsmith's art of the time had been raised by the influences alluded to.

Perhaps the one place which retains in the most varied and concentrated form the traces of this wave of artistic development then passing over Germany, is Hildesheim. This is of interest here because the bishops of Hildesheim were specially appointed to perform the office of consecration of nuns at Gandersheim. It seems hardly possible that Roswitha could have seen its gifted bishop Bernward, himself a painter, and a worker in mosaic and metals, though owing to the uncertainty of the date of her death—one chronicler making it as late as 1002—it is just possible that she may have done so. Bernward's learning and artistic nature attracted the attention of the princess Theophano, who appointed him tutor to her son, the boy-emperor Otho the Third. Brought thus into touch with the many gifts presented on special occasions to the young Emperor by Greek and Oriental princes, as well as by "Scots" (*i.e.* Irish missionaries and emigrants settled in Germany), he, by taking with him to Court, from the School of Art established in his palace at Hildesheim, apt and talented youths, made use of these rare and beautiful offerings for the encouragement of the study of divers arts. Students also accompanied him when he went farther afield for study, for it is said of him that there was no art which he did not attempt, even if he failed to attain perfection.[1] Hildesheim thus became famous as a working-centre of fine art, especially in metals, and remained so down to the end of the Middle Ages. After a lapse of nearly a thousand years, the result of the labours of this artistic prelate and his pupils

[1] Thangmarus, "Vita Sti. Bernwardi," Migne, *Patrol. Lat.* 140, col. 397. 6.

may still be seen in situ as it were. Besides jewelled service-books, there are chalices, incense burners, a gold candelabrum, and a jewelled crucifix, fashioned, if not in part by him, at least under his supervision. The entrance to the Cathedral is beautified with delicately wrought bronze doors, modelled, it may be, from those of Sta. Sabina, Rome, themselves considered to be of Oriental origin,[1] and in the transept rises a column adorned with bronze reliefs from the life of Christ, probably designed by the bishop either after his pilgrimage to Rome in 1001, when he had seen Trajan's column, or, as a recent writer suggests, from the "Juppiter and giant columns" of Roman Rhineland.[2]

We are tempted to recall other princesses whose marriages, and even more whose personalities, have influenced art and letters, but two must suffice us — the one, the beautiful and cultivated Anne of Bohemia, wife of Richard the Second, whose bridal retinue was in reality a small Court of literary and artistic personages ; the other, the brilliant Valentine Visconti of Milan, sister-in-law of King Charles the Sixth of France, whose influence in matters of art and literature alone, at a time when England and France were so intimately associated, makes her of special interest to us.

[1] Michel, *Histoire de l'Art*, 1905, Tome I. i. p. 258.
[2] *Journal of Roman Studies*, vol. i. part i., 1911, article by E. Strong, p. 24.

But what bearing, it may be asked, had Court life on the life of the nun Roswitha in the convent of Gandersheim ? To answer this question we must recall briefly the position of the early religious houses, and especially those of Saxony. Many of the foundations were royal, and, in return for certain privileges, were obliged to entertain the king and his retinue whenever he journeyed. Such sojourns naturally brought a store of political, intellectual, and other information to the favoured house. Added to this, the abbess of such a house, generally a highborn and influential woman, was, in her position as a ruler of lands as well as of communities, brought into direct contact with the Court and with politics. To her rights of overlordship were attached the same privileges and duties as in the case of any feudal baron. She issued summonses for attendance at her Courts, at which she was represented by a proctor, and, when war was declared, she had to provide the prescribed number of knights. In some cases her influence was supreme, even in imperial affairs, extending also to matters social and literary. Roswitha tells us how much she herself owed to the two successive abbesses under whose rule she lived, for suggestion, information, and encouragement in her literary work.

The convents of Saxony, as many elsewhere in the tenth and eleventh centuries, were centres of culture in the nature of endowed colleges.

In some of them women resided permanently, and besides their religious exercises, devoted themselves to learning and the arts, for the Church of the Middle Ages took thought for the intellect as well as for the soul. In others, no irrevocable vows were made, and if desire or necessity arose, the student inmate was free to return to the world. In others again, though residence was permanent, short leave of absence from time to time was granted by the abbess, and the nun was able to sojourn with her friends, or to visit some sister community. But at Gandersheim the rule was strict, and a nun, her vows once taken, had to remain within the convent walls. Yet even so, life there was perhaps far less circumscribed than in many a castle, where the men gave themselves up to war and the chase, and the women perforce spun and embroidered and gossiped, since to venture without the walls was fraught with difficulty and sometimes with danger. Even if there were some who cared to read, and who would fain go in imagination to other scenes and times, MSS. were difficult to come by, and costly withal. Wholly different was it in the religious houses. In these, women associated with their equals, with whom they could interchange ideas, and the library was well furnished with MSS. of classical and Christian writers. One of the first cares of St. Benedict, in the case of every newly founded house, was the formation of the library. So held in honour did this tradition become, and so assiduously was it pursued, that the status of a monastery or a convent, as a centre of learning, came to be estimated by its wealth in MSS. Besides the mass of transcribing which such rivalry occasioned, there was illuminating to be done, musical notation to be studied and prepared for the services of the Church, chants and choir-singing to be practised, and the needful time to be devoted to weaving and embroidery—a part of every woman's education. Weaving had of necessity to be done in every convent in order to provide the requisite clothing for its inmates, and the large and often elaborate hangings used for covering the walls. Embroidery, on the other hand, was no mere occupation, or even a craft, but in truth a fine art. The few specimens still preserved give some idea of the quality of the work, whilst old inventories attest the quantity. Illuminated MSS. of the Gospels and the Apocalypse were lent from royal treasuries, and their miniatures were copied, with needle and silk, to adorn vestments and altar hangings. Then at Gandersheim, as we have already said, the occasional visits of princely travellers brought interest and diversion from the outside world. It was in an atmosphere such as this that Roswitha passed her days.

Of her work, the metrical legends seem her earliest effort. In these, though they are mainly based on well-known themes, Roswitha shows much originality in description. Whilst they need not detain us, passing reference may be made to two of them—the Passion of St. Pelagius of Cordova, and the Fall and Conversion of Theophilus—since their subject matter is of value to us to-day. The one interests us because, in relating that the story was told her by an eye-witness of the martyrdom in A.D. 925 (*Acta SS.* Jun. V.), she shows that communication existed between that great intellectual centre, Cordova, and Germany, a fact that must have had considerable influence on art and literature ; the other as being the story out of which the Faust legend was developed.

After these legends, we turn to her panegyric on the Emperor Otho. This she opens by acknowledging her debt to the Abbess Gerberg, niece of Otho the Great, for aiding her in her literary work with her superior knowledge, and for giving her the necessary information concerning the royal doings. Then by humbly likening her mental perplexity and fear on entering upon so vast a subject to the feelings of one who has to cross a forest in winter when snow has obliterated the track, she in a few words pictures for us the natural wooded surroundings of the convent. Her poem—for such it really is—then sets forth the personal history of this monarch and his predecessors, rather than public events, and is thus of value more on account of its poetical than its historical quality. But one episode, picturesque in its quaint setting, and interesting historically because its stirring details are not to be found elsewhere, is worthy

of record. It centres round Adelheid, the young
and beautiful widow of Lothair, a Lombard king.
Taken prisoner by his successor, the tyrant
Berengarius, she is immured in a castle on the
Lago di Garda, and threatened with a forced
marriage with the son of her oppressor. This
threat seems to endow her with superhuman
power. Bidding defiance to all difficulty and
danger, she contrives gradually to dig a secret
way through the soft earth, and suddenly finds
herself free. Dawn is just breaking. But how
can she make use of her freedom before her
guards awake and discover her escape ? Quickly
is her mind made up. But let Roswitha herself
tell the story :—

As soon as black night yielded to the twilight, and the
heavens began to pale before the rays of the sun, warily hiding
herself in secluded caves, now she wanders in the woods, now
lurks in the furrows amongst the ripe ears of Ceres, until
returning night, clothed in its wonted gloom, again veils the
earth in darkness. Then once more is she diligent to pursue
her way begun. And her guards, not finding her, all-trembling
make it known to the officer charged with the safe keeping of
the lady. And he, struck to the heart with the terror of
grievous fear, set forth with much company to make diligent
search for her, and when he failed, and moreover could not discover whither the most illustrious queen had turned her steps,
fearful, he made report of the matter to King Berengarius.
And he, at once filled with exceeding wrath, forthwith sent
his dependants everywhere around, commanding them not to
overlook any small place, but cautiously to examine every
hiding-place, lest perchance the queen might be lying hid in
any an one. And he himself followed with a band of stout-
hearted troops as if to overcome some fierce enemy in battle.
And rapidly did he pass on his way through the self-same
corn-field in the which the lady whom he sought was lurking

in the bent-back furrows, hidden beneath the wings of Ceres. Hither and thither forsooth he traversed the very spot where she lay, burdened with no little fear, and although, with great effort, he essayed with outstretched spear to part the corn around, yet he discovered not her whom by the grace of Christ it concealed.

From the sheltering corn Adelheid effects her escape, and after weary wandering, reaches the Castle of Canossa, the stronghold of the Counts of Tuscany. Any one who has visited this now ruined castle, some twenty miles from Parma, will remember the threadlike way between rocks covered with brambles, by which its eyrie height is approached. Up this steep track the queen, fearful of any pause, hastens, and finds a welcome and ready help. The Count becomes her champion, and appeals on her behalf to the Emperor Otho. The latter, glad of an excuse to further his cause in Italy, descends with his troops into the Lombard plain, weds the beautiful Adelheid, and receives the formal cession of the so-called kingdom of Italy from Berengarius and his son, whose power had ebbed away in their futile attempts to control their feudatories.

Roswitha's thrilling narrative is amplified by the graphic account recorded by St. Odilo, Abbot of Cluny, Queen Adelheid's friend and one-time confessor. In this he tells us that during Adelheid's imprisonment in a castle on the Lago di Garda, her chaplain Martin succeeds in making a hole in the wall, through which the queen and her maidservant, disguised as men, creep. He does not recount the episode of the hiding in the corn, but relates another equally stirring adventure. He tells us that, in fleeing from their persecutor to the safety of Canossa, the fugitives become involved in a swamp. After two days, they are rescued from their perilous position by a fisherman who, passing near by, and hearing sounds of distress, goes to their aid. Their deliverer, finding them faint with hunger and cold, lights a fire with the flint he carries in his wallet, and cooks some small fish, the only food he has to offer them. Once more they start on their way, and eventually reach Canossa. But hardly do they gain admittance, ere the castle is surrounded by the soldiery of the outwitted and wrathful Berengarius. A knight, carrying a message from the Emperor Otho of promised deliverance, essays to enter the castle, but finding this impossible owing to the hostile troops encamped around, he fastens the letter to an arrow, and shoots it over the wall. A strong force sent by Otho is near at hand, and speedily puts the enemy to flight. Adelheid is rescued, and is brought with rejoicing to Pavia, her dower city, which had already opened its gates to the Emperor, and she and the Emperor enter the city together in triumph. Much has been written of the illustrious Adelheid, but perhaps she would best like to be remembered by the eulogy of her confessor —the saintly Odilo—that she never forgot a kindness, or remembered an injury.

ROSWITHA THE NUN

It is in a spirit far different from that of her panegyric on the emperor Otho that Roswitha writes her dramas. Fear and mental perplexity no longer possess her. Though humbly begging the reader not to "despise these strains drawn from a fragile reed," she has no misgiving, for she feels that herein lies her mission. She explains her reason for using the dramatic form, and for taking Terence as her model. There are many, she says,—and she does not entirely exonerate herself,—who, beguiled by the elegant diction of the Classics, prefer them to religious writings, whilst there are others who, though generally condemning heathen works, eagerly peruse the poetic creations of Terence because of the special beauty of his language. She further expresses the hope that by trying to imitate his manner, and by at the same time dramatising legends calculated to edify, she may induce readers to turn from the "godless contents of his works" to the contemplation of virtuous living. Emboldened by this pious hope, Roswitha shrinks from no difficulties or details, details which might well have made her hesitate, and which, betraying a knowledge of the world, have raised the question as to whether she made her profession as early as was customary. This solicitude of Roswitha for the welfare of frail and all too human mankind recalls St. Bernard's condemnation, some hundred and fifty years later, of all carving in church or cloister, when he says, "one reads with more pleasure what is carven in stones than what is written in books, and would rather gaze all day upon these singular creations than meditate upon the Divine Word."

It has been maintained that the classic theatre decayed and disappeared as Christianity became all-powerful in Europe, and that the modern theatre seemingly arose in the twelfth century out of the services of the Church, and owed no debt to the past. But neither Nature nor Art works in this way except to our own unperceiving minds. After the fall of the Roman Empire, and the consequent disruption of society, classic civilisation gradually withdrew into the security of the religious communities, seeking, like distraught humanity, shelter and protection. It was in such tranquil atmosphere as this that Latin drama, though condemned in substance, was fostered and favoured as an education in style. Roswitha's plays may, as has been said, have been the last ray of classical antiquity, but if so, it was a ray, like the pillar of fire, bright enough to guide through the dark night of feudalism to the coming day.

Whether her dramatic efforts were an isolated phenomenon or not, must remain undecided, but it is reasonable to assume that any work surviving to the present day is but a sample of much else of the same sort that has disappeared in the course of time. Still all we would claim for them, apart from their intrinsic value and interest, is that they helped to keep up continuity in the tradition of drama. The gradual movement in the Church towards elaboration in its services which began in the ninth century,—a movement which led to the dramatising of the Mass, out of which the liturgical drama, and eventually the miracle-play, were evolved,—was a popular movement. To a people ignorant of Latin, yet fond of shows, it provided instruction and diversion alike. Roswitha, on the other hand, avowedly wrote for the literary world, and with a special end in view as regards that world. To attain this end, she set before her, as her master in style, Terence, who himself had aimed at a high ideal of artistic perfection, and of whom it has been said that he perpetuated the art and genius of Menander just as a master engraver perpetuates the designs of a great painter whose works have since perished. Still, in spite of the glamour of the style to which she aspires, and poetess though she is by nature, her plays reflect the handiwork of the moralist rather than that of the artist, for though beauty charms her by the way, her goal is moral truth, and to this all else must yield. If we would see the beauty of holiness as she saw it, we must enter in spirit within the shrine of her thought and feeling, just as the traveller, standing without the simple brick exterior of the tomb of Galla Placidia, at Ravenna, must penetrate within if he would know of the beauty there enshrined. "Il faut être saint, pour comprendre la sainteté."

The subject which dominates her horizon is that of Chastity. Treated by her with didactic intent, this really resolves itself into a conflict between Christianity and Paganism,—in other words, between Chastity and Passion,—in which Christianity triumphs through the virtue of Woman. But at the same time Roswitha neither contemns marriage nor generally advocates celibacy. She merely counsels, as the more blessed, the unmarried state. Yet even so, we feel that beneath her nun's garb there beats the heart of a sympathetic woman, whose emotional self-expression is but tempered by the ideals of her time and her surroundings.

Another important element to be taken into account in her plays is the part she assigns to the supernatural. It is impossible to develop character with any continuity when the supernatural, like some sword of Damocles, hovers continually overhead, ready to descend at any moment and sever cause from effect. Such a sword was the Divine Presence to Roswitha. When her plot requires it, she introduces a miracle, converting a character, at a moment's notice, and in a way that no evolution could possibly effect, into one of a totally different kind. Still to her audience such a *dénouement* would be quite satisfactory. With her, sudden changes and conversions but reflect the ideas which possessed the minds of her contemporaries, who realised God more in deviations from, than in manifestations of, law and order.

ROSWITHA THE NUN

Were her plays ever performed? To this question no certain answer can be given, since no record has yet been found of their performance, and the best critics are at variance on the subject. But judging from analogy, there seems to be no reason why they should not have been. We know that as early as the fifth and sixth centuries the monks played Terence, probably on some fête-day, or before their scholars as a means of instruction, and doubtless Roswitha's plays were also acted on special occasions, such as when the Emperor sojourned at Gandersheim, or the Bishop made a visitation. As they were written in Latin, the literary language of the time, this in itself, even if their themes had appealed to the people, would have prevented them from being performed save before the educated few. So if we would picture to ourselves a performance of one of them by her companion nuns in the Chapter House, or it may be in the refectory, it must be before the Bishop and his clergy, and perhaps also some members of the Imperial family, and lords and ladies of the Court. How refreshing must such an entertainment have been to this distinguished company as it found itself carried away into an atmosphere of poetry and passion, of movement and colour, in place of the sobriety induced by the stiff liturgical dramas that probably formed the usual diversion! Such a drama was that of *The Wise and Foolish Virgins*, a specially favourite old-world dramatic exercise, dispensed as a sort of religious tonic to womankind, calculated to arouse slumbering souls, or to quicken to still further effort those that did not slumber. For us, its chief interest lies in the antiphonic arrangement of the dialogue, in which we may trace the first germs of characterisation, and in the music, the refrains of which contain the first suggestions, as far as we know, of the principle of the leitmotiv, a principle carried to its most complete development by Wagner. Although the earliest known MS. of it is of the eleventh century, so finished, yet so simple, are its dialogues and refrains, that it seems not unreasonable to infer that the form of the play was well known, either through some earlier MS. or through oral tradition. It is only a slight development of the elegy in dialogue which was performed in A.D. 874, at the funeral of Hathumoda, the first abbess of Gandersheim. This dialogue takes place between the sorrow-stricken nuns, who speak in chorus of their loss, and the monk Wichbert, who acts as consoler. Although its form is liturgical, its subject entitles it to be considered the earliest known mediæval dramatic work extant.

Of Roswitha's dramas, three seem to stand out as of special interest—*Abraham*, *Callimachus*, and *Paphnutius*. All of these are more or less patchwork adaptations from the legendary débris of antiquity. The first appears to have been taken by Roswitha from a Latin translation of a

fourth-century Greek legend.[1] Whilst she does
not display any originality in elaborating the
story, but keeps carefully to the text—so much
so that at times she merely transcribes—she
reveals her artistic as well as her psychological
instinct by concentrating the essentials, thereby
transforming a rather discursive composition into
a poignant picture. The subtle touches, the
sentiment, and the dialogue so pathetic and so
true to nature, make this drama verily her
masterpiece, and one worthy of a place beside
the delicate and dramatic miniatures of the time.
In a few words, here is the story. A holy man,
by name Abraham, has abandoned a life of solitude in order to take care of his young orphaned
niece. After a few years, she is tempted to a
house of ill fame. Some two years later, her
uncle, having discovered her whereabouts, determines to exchange his hermit garb for that of a
man of the world, and go to the house in the
guise of a lover, so as to get an opportunity of
speaking with his niece alone. Of course she
does not recognise him in his change of costume,
and when he asks for a kiss, she puts her arms
round his neck, and suddenly detects a strange
perfume. Instantly a change comes over her.
The scent recalls to her her former unsullied life,
and tears fill her eyes. At the fitting moment
the uncle makes himself known, and showing
her with sweet words of sympathy and encouragement that sin is natural to humanity, and that

[1] Migne, *Patrol. Lat.* lxxiii.

what is evil is to continue in it, takes her back
with him to begin afresh the simple good life.

The second play recounts an incident taken
from the apocryphal Acts of the Apostles, supposed to take place in the first century. A young
heathen, Callimachus, falls in love with a young
married woman, a Christian. She dies, and is
buried the same day. That night Callimachus
goes to the grave, and with the help of a slave
disinters the body. Holding it in his arms, and
triumphing in the embrace denied to him in life,
he suddenly falls dead. In the morning the
husband and St. John, coming to the cemetery
to pray for her soul, see the rifled grave and the
two dead bodies. St. John, at the command of
Christ, who appears for but a moment, restores
them both to life, and brings to repentance the
young man, who, in further amendment of his
ways, becomes a Christian. This mere outline of
the play is given to suggest points of resemblance
between it—the first sketch of this kind of drama
of passion, the frenzy of the soul and senses—and
the masterpiece of this type, *Romeo and Juliet.*

Many passages in the plays of Roswitha
remind us of Shakespeare, but it is not possible
to deal adequately with them here, nor does it
seem material to do so. There is no reason why
Shakespeare should not have seen a printed
collection of her dramas. He, like Dante,
seems to have had the power of attracting
material from every possible source, and it should
not be forgotten what a sensation was caused by

Celtes printing in 1501 Roswitha's MS. But, on the other hand, the similarities we notice may be a mere coincidence, or, as is much more likely, the details in each case may have been common property handed down from one generation to another.

In her play of *Paphnutius*, Roswitha made use of a story taken from the *Historia Monachorum* of Rufinus, a contemporary of St. Jerome, who had journeyed through Palestine and Egypt to visit the Hermits of the Desert. The mention, too, at the beginning of Rufinus's account, of a musician who tells of his retirement to a hermitage in order to change the harmony of music into that of the spirit, evidently suggested to her a discussion on music and harmony, probably adapted from Boëthius's *De Musica*. In this discussion lies the chief interest of the play as giving us some idea of the sort of intellectual exercises probably practised by women in convents in the tenth century. The play opens with a truly mediæval scene,—a disputation between a hermit and his disciples on the question of harmony between soul and body, suggested by the want of it in the life of the courtesan Thais. Such harmony *should* exist, says the holy man, for though the soul is not mortal like the body, nor the body spiritual like the soul, we shall, if we follow the method of the dialecticians, find that such differences do not necessarily render the two inharmonious. Harmony cannot be produced from like elements or like sounds, but only by the right adjustment of those which are dissimilar. This discussion on harmony naturally leads to one on music, which is divided, according to the then received writers on the subject, into three kinds—celestial, human, and instrumental. Music, in the Middle Ages, was, for dialectical purposes, treated in accordance with the Pythagorean theory as interpreted by Cicero in his *Somnium Scipionis*, who represented the eight revolving spheres of heaven—the Earth being fixed—as forming a complete musical octave. Such celestial music forms the subject of the argument in Roswitha's play, the music of Earth being merely touched upon. Why, it is asked, do we not hear this music of the spheres if it exists? To this comes the answer that some think it is because of its continuity, others because of the density of the atmosphere, and others again because the volume of sound cannot penetrate the narrow passage of the human ear. And so with subtle argument, the music of Heaven was often drowned in the din of Earth. Dante, in the *Paradiso*, lifted the idea once more from Earth to Heaven, and clothed it in a wealth of gorgeous imagery. But it is Shakespeare who, with the magic of a few words, has given the thought immortality.

> There's not the smallest orb which thou behold'st
> But in his motion like an angel sings,
>
> . . . . . .
>
> Such harmony is in immortal souls ;
> But whilst this muddy vesture of decay
> Doth grossly close it in, we cannot hear it.

26

ROSWITHA THE NUN

In judging of Roswitha's dramatic work it must be remembered that, in true mediæval spirit fearing to profane what she venerates, she allows herself but little licence with the legends she dramatises. Nevertheless, as has been said, she from time to time shows, in psychological touches, a capacity for originality quite phenomenal for her time and for the literature of the cloister. Still her plays express but a very small part of the whole gamut of human emotions and experiences, just as her life was lived in an intellectual world narrow from the point of view of to-day or of the great intellectual age of antiquity. Many causes contributed to this. Intellectually, the Christian world shrank as Paganism was superseded by Christianity, a supersession by no means complete in Roswitha's day. Of course this nascent Christianity was inconsistent with much of the intellectual life of the ancient world, which was either inextricably interwoven with Paganism, or essentially anti-religious. With its task of laying afresh the foundations of education, politics, and morality, it had to take root and become established in a relatively narrow intellectual field, the boundaries of which had gradually to be broken down, sometimes with violence.

Time, like some lens which clears our vision, makes it an easy task to criticise and condemn a phase of religious life which, having essayed to tranquillise and sweeten existence, was, under altered conditions of civilisation, bound to pass away. We of to-day pride ourselves on a wider view of life, on a higher conception of duty, expressed in lives dedicated to public work as a necessary complement to private virtue. Still, if we would judge fairly this age of contemplation and faith within the convent walls, and all that, even if done mistakenly and imperfectly, it aspired to do, we must realise, as best we can, the world without those walls. One of our poets has vividly reflected it for us when he speaks of man's life as made up of "whole centuries of folly, noise, and sin." So bitter was life then and even later, that by the thirteenth and fourteenth centuries, when mysticism had claimed many votaries, eternal rest, even at the cost of personal annihilation, was the whispered desire of many devout souls.

" A Simple Stillness." " An Eternal Silence." These are the words that float across the centuries to us, like echoes from troubled, longing hearts. These are the words that give us the key to the understanding of the choice of vocation of the mediæval woman. The spiritual need for harmony and peace may have been great ; the practical need was perhaps even greater ; for in its accomplishment the spiritual found its consummation.

A TWELFTH-CENTURY ROMANCE-
WRITER,
MARIE DE FRANCE

" Marie ai nom, si sui de France." Thus, more
than seven centuries ago, wrote Marie de France.
What an unpretentious autobiography! Yet
these few simple words, which seem to tell so
little, but in reality suggest so much, are the
counterpart of her work, and form its fitting
crown.

But who was this modest writer, and why does
her work interest us to-day? Around Marie de
France there must always remain an atmosphere
of doubt and mystery, since she is only mentioned by an anonymous thirteenth-century poet,
and by one of her contemporaries—an Anglo-
Norman poet, Denys Pyramus by name—who
speaks of her in the most flattering terms, and
from whom we learn that her lays were much
appreciated by the noblesse, especially the ladies.
That these should take rare delight in them
may well be, seeing how monotonous life must
have been to many a woman shut up with her
maidens and her needlework in a dismal castle,

29

or perhaps in but one tower of it, whilst her lord went forth to the chase or to war, his home-coming meaning merely the wine-cup and war-songs, or tedious epic. Many a one must have read or listened to Marie's love idylls, and longed, and perhaps even hoped, as in the story of "Yonec," that a fair and gentle knight, in the form of some beautiful bird, might fly in at her window and bring her some diversion from the outside world. With nothing before us but her own poems and the scant recognition of Denys Pyramus, she seems like some old portrait in which the delicate pigments that once glowed in the face and made it live have, owing to their very delicacy, long since faded away, leaving behind only the stronger and less volatile colours of the dark background from which we in vain try to wrest more than one or two fragments of the secret it holds.

Judging from internal evidence, it would seem that Marie was born in Normandy, about the middle of the twelfth century, but settled in England, where since the Conquest, and indeed since the time of Edward the Confessor, many Norman families had made their home. Not only does she make occasional use of English words, and translate from English into French the fables known as Æsop's, but in the prologue to her *Lays*, which she dedicates to "the noble King," generally considered to be Henry the Second, she expresses fear lest her work should not find favour in a foreign land. In this prologue she

also gives her reason for abandoning classical
translation, which, as a Latin scholar, she had
contemplated making, not only for the use of the
less learned, but also, as she tells us, for personal
discipline, since " he who would keep himself
from sin, should study and learn and undertake
difficult tasks. In suchwise he may the more
withdraw him and save himself from much
sorrow." The twelfth century was a time of
extraordinary intellectual activity, and Marie
tells us that she suffered from what we are apt
to regard as a special evil of our own day—the
overcrowding of the literary market. So she
wisely turned aside from the Classics and the
crowd, and set herself to give literary expression
to the old Celtic folk-lore, hitherto perhaps
unrecorded save in song.

Of Marie's work that has come down to
us we have *The Fables*, already mentioned,
dedicated to Count William, surnamed Long-
sword, and son of Henry the Second and Fair
Rosamond;[1] *The Lays*, dedicated to the king,
Henry the Second, and doubtless read by Fair
Rosamond in her retreat at Woodstock ; and
The Purgatory of St. Patrick, translated from the
Latin at the request of an anonymous bene-
factor. Of these only *The Lays* need here concern us, as it is in them that our interest lies,

---

[1] Marie thus refers to Count William :—

"Pur amur le cumte Willaume,
Le plus vaillant de cest royaume,
M'entremis de cest livre feire,
E de l'Angleiz en Roman treire."

since they are perhaps among the first stories, given literary form, which tell of love "for love's sake only,"—love unqualified and unquestioning. They form, perhaps, the only collection of lays now extant, and it is to them, therefore, that we must turn to get some idea of the style of narration that gradually replaced the taste for the epic as Norman influence grew and spread in England. Beside the sensualism of the *Chansons de Geste*, the sentiment expressed in them may seem naïve ; beside the gallantry of the Provençal poetry, it may seem primitive ; but nevertheless it is, in its very simplicity, the profoundest note that can be struck in this world of men and women. Marie makes no pretence to originality, but even if she did not possess the supreme gift of creating beauty, she at least possessed the lesser gift of perceiving it where it existed and of making it her own, and her stories glow with colour, and enchant by their simple yet dramatic appeal to the imagination. She declares that *The Lays* were made "for remembrance" by "Le ancien Bretun curteis," and that "Folks tell them to the harp and the rote, and the music is sweet to hear." Doubtless it was this sweet music which both soothed and thrilled even before the words were understood, for on sad and festive days alike, the sweet lays of Brittany were always to be heard.

La reine chante doucement,
La voiz acorde a l'estrument :
Les mains sont belles, li lais bons,
Douce la voiz et bas li tons.

LADY PLAYING HARP.

Add. MS. 38117, Brit. Mus.

To face page 32.

MARIE DE FRANCE

Whether Marie was connected with the Court of Henry the Second and his brilliant and artistic queen, Eleanor of Aquitaine, where learned men and poets congregated, we do not know, but it seems a very fair conjecture that she was. Not only does she dedicate her principal work to the king and his son, Count William, but her stories are coloured with the courtly life and ideas of her time, notwithstanding the simplicity of the fundamental theme. It is doubtful whether any one unacquainted with the teaching of the Courts of Love, such as they were in the twelfth century, would have made the compulsory quest of love the keynote of a story, as, for instance, Marie does in the " Lay of Guigemar." These Courts of Love, though not so elaborate, yet seemingly as imperious, as those of the fourteenth century, formed one of the semi-serious pastimes of the Middle Ages, and although it may be that they were often mere forms of entertainment, no self-respecting person could afford to disregard their rules or decisions. The cardinal doctrine was that love was necessary to a man's moral, social, and æsthetic training. Hence if it did not arise of itself, it must be sought for, and, like its counterpart in the spiritual world, come at, if needs be, through much tribulation.

Owing to Henry's possessions in France through inheritance, marriage, and the many ties of relationship which united the royal families of both countries, England and France were never more closely allied than they were at that time. French was established by them as the speech of the cultured and the high-born. The Norman Conquest had made us more cosmopolitan in both manners and ideas. May we not look on the victory at Hastings as a symbol as well as a reality ? Did it not mean for us a spiritual as well as a material conquest, since, mingled with the clashing of battle-axes, was to be heard the chanting of the *Chanson de Roland* ? Moreover, through a desire to bring about uniformity of sentiment and service, the Church, though perhaps unconsciously, aided this good work of general enlargement of outlook by appointing outsiders to control our abbeys and religious foundations. Thus, in the latter half of the twelfth century, the romantic movement which characterised late mediæval literature stirred in England and France alike, and Marie was one of its truest and daintiest exponents. Although what she relates may be fiction intermingled with myth and magic, she all the same pictures on her somewhat small canvases the ideas of her time, and so helps to make history.

Marie's readers and hearers were naturally to be found amongst castle-folk. That these were many we may conclude from the fact that the number of castles had already come to be regarded as a menace to the central government, and a royal command had gone forth for the demolition of many of them. That her stories

ADD. MS. 10293, BRIT. MUS.

To face page 34.

were read and prized for at least a century and more is evident from the manuscripts—five in number, and all of the thirteenth, or the beginning of the fourteenth, century—which still exist. Her renown, too, had travelled even beyond the seas, for in about A.D. 1245 a translation of her lays into Norse was made by order of the king, Haakon the Fourth. The fact that their popularity began to wane after a hundred years or so is in no wise an adverse criticism of their intrinsic worth, for in the fourteenth century English was, in high places, beginning to take the place of French, and naturally the demand created a supply. But even if this had not been so, Marie's work had served its purpose, and of necessity passed into the crucible of human thought and expression, to be resolved into matter suited to other needs and conditions. As has been well said, "les siècles se succèdent, et chacun porte son fruit, qui n'est pas celui du siècle précédent : les livres sont les fruits des mœurs."

Of the five manuscripts still extant, two are in the British Museum. One of these is the most complete that has come down to us, seeing that, in addition to its including the largest number of lays—twelve in all,—it alone contains the prologue, in which for a moment the illusive Marie lifts, as it were, her all-enshrouding veil. It is a small manuscript, beautifully inscribed, and even after its seven hundred years of existence, as fresh as is the love enshrined in its parchment pages. How strange a feeling possesses us as we turn over its leaves, leaves across which the shadows of readers of bygone days still seem to flit ! Could these pages speak, of what would they tell ? Of desires that die not, of longings that are immortal, of love enthroned.

When first read, these stories, so simply are they told, may seem somewhat slight and superficial. But this is the general characteristic of mediæval literature, which, for the most part, recognised things in outline only, and sought, and perhaps possessed, but little knowledge of the hidden springs of motive. The writers of those times troubled as little about moral, as the early painters did about physical, anatomy. Still, in spite of this indifference to what has become almost a craze in our own day, Marie's lays are so full of charming detail, deftly handled, that they give much the same sense of delight as do delicate ivories or dainty embroidery. Sometimes, it is true, she scarcely, despite all this outward charm, seems to touch the world of fact. Yet in this ideal atmosphere which she so essentially made her own, she contrives to convey such a sense of reality, that for the moment we are wholly possessed by it and carried away, without questioning, into her fairyland. And a beautiful fairyland it is, where love triumphs for the most part, not in heedless ecstasy along flower-bestrewn ways, but through self-sacrifice and suffering mutually accepted and mutually endured. Listen to the words spoken to the knight Guigemar, wounded by a chance arrow as he rides through a wood. " Never shalt thou be healed of thy wound, not even by herb, or root, or leach, or potion, until thou art healed by her who, for love of thee, shall suffer such great pain and sorrow as never woman has suffered before : and thou shalt bear as much for her." Equality in love ! Such is the vital note struck amid the artificial and soul-enfeebling atmosphere of mediæval love-poetry ! This is the note which Marie set ringing down the centuries whilst her manuscripts lay unused on library shelves. This is Marie's gift to the world, and this it is that gives her stories immortality. Not only do they possess this immortality in themselves, but they have also been immortalised by poets and writers both in days long past and in those more within our ken. All who know her stories will recall Chaucer's indebtedness to incidents and descriptions in them, and coming to our own time, we find Sir Walter Scott taking his ballad of " Lord Thomas and Fair Annie " from the lay of " The Ash Tree," although it is possible, as has been suggested,[1] that his ballad may have been founded on some Scotch folk-song having a common origin with Marie's lay. When her lays were first published in Germany in 1820, Goethe wrote thus : " The mist of years that mysteriously envelops Marie de France makes her poems more exquisite and

[1] Warnke. *Die lais der Marie de France*, p. lxiii.

precious to us." Yes, it is this all-pervading mystery which, though so tantalising, is yet so attractive. It is in vain that, in studying them, we try to penetrate somewhat beyond our normal atmosphere, for we only find ourselves lost in vague possibilities and hazy distances. Brittany has kept her secret concerning such of these lays as were hers just as jealously as she has kept her secret of the long avenues of great lichened stones which make Carnac look like the burial-place of some giant host. Marie's lays are stories of deep meaning, which each reader must interpret for himself.

It is impossible to do more here than just touch upon Marie's ideal conception of love, for to realise it fully it is necessary to read the stories themselves.[1] Allusion has been made to the wounded knight in the " Lay of Guigemar," who can only be healed through mutual love sanctified by mutual suffering. In the lay of "The Ash Tree" a maiden of noble birth, abandoned in infancy and brought up in a convent, is loved by a lord, and returns his love, and goes with him to his castle. After a time the knights who owe him fealty complain that as through his love for his mistress he has neither wife nor child, he does them wrong, and protest that if he does not wed some noble lady, they will no longer serve him or hold him for

[1] Marie de France, *Seven of her Lays*, trans. E. Sickert, 1901 ; Warnke, *Die lais der Marie de France*, Halle, 1885 ; Hertz, *Spielmannsbuch*, 1905.

lord. The knight has to yield to their demands and to consent to accept in marriage the daughter of a neighbouring noble who had made it known that he desired him for son-in-law. Neither lover utters any complaint or reproach, and the needful sacrifice is about to be made. But fortune, sometimes kind, intervenes ere it is too late, and reveals the noble birth of the loved one. The knight weds her with great joy, and to complete this happy picture we read that the other lady returned with her parents to her own domain, and was there well bestowed in marriage.

This idea of mutual sympathy and sacrifice gives meaning also to the lay of " The Two Lovers," and to that of " Yonec," but perhaps it is most simply, yet forcibly, summed up in the lay of " The Honeysuckle," an episode taken from the Tristan story. Tristan, hearing that Isolde is to ride through a certain wood on her way to Tintagel to attend the Pentecostal Court held by the King, hides in the wood. Here he cuts a branch of hazel round which honeysuckle has twined, and carving his name and certain letters on it, he lays it in the way by which the Queen must pass, knowing that she will recognise it as a sign that her lover is near, since they have met before in suchwise. The import of the writing is that he has long been waiting to see her, since without her he cannot live, and that they two are like the hazel branch with the encircling honeysuckle, the which, as long as they are intertwined, thrive, but as soon as they are separated, both perish. Says Tristan, "Sweet Love, so is it with us—nor you without me, nor I without you."

But besides this conception of love which Marie had simply found awaiting expression, when we turn to examine the stories somewhat in detail, we find legend and poetry, Eastern magic and Christian symbolism, mingled with strange ingenuity. Whence came all these divers threads which Marie has so dexterously interwoven? It is very difficult to tell whether we are wholly in a world of romance, accepted by her without question, or whether she had some understanding of the divers matters she touches upon, and shaped them into a new form to suit new hearers. The answer to this question seems to depend on whether Marie recounted the lays from hearsay, or whether they had been already written down, and were merely retold by her, she colouring them with the atmosphere of her time, which was charged with strange incongruities of religion and magic. To this we can give no certain answer, since Marie herself gives no hint, and only tells us that the ancient Bretons made the lays. But whatever may have been her contribution, Christian or otherwise, to the original matter she worked upon, we cannot help feeling that we have before us the remains of some primitive mythology overlaid and interpenetrated with Eastern lore, especially that of India, which, in the Middle Ages, was spread broadcast in the West. This Indian thought, itself borrowed in a measure from Egypt, had also been tempered by the Hellenism which, after the conquests of Alexander the Great in Asia, had filtered through India, and had on the way become tinged with its colour and its mystery. It was from the matter of these Indian stories that so much was learnt, for whilst, in the West, the national epic and the chivalrous romance had been alone considered worthy of record, in the Indian stories all social conditions were revealed, and poets thus learnt little by little to observe and portray the manners and sentiments of the people generally, changing social conditions also acting in the same direction. All such influences must be taken into consideration in studying mediæval literature generally, but particularly the occult element in Oriental thought which presents such difficulties to the less meditative Western mind, and has in consequence given rise to much misconception.

In the "Lay of Guigemar," which we take first because it is the first in the manuscript, we find Marie making use of a subject, in gorgeous setting, of Christian symbolism, but using it apparently so unconsciously that it is only from one or two details that we realise what is really lurking in disguise. Guigemar, the wounded knight already referred to, to whom naught but love, and sorrow endured for love, can bring any alleviation, sets forth for his healing. He comes across a ship into which he enters, and which by unseen means carries him to the desired haven. As we read the description of the ship, our thoughts at once revert to the picture of the barge in which Cleopatra goes to meet Antony. Marie tells us that the fittings are of ebony, and the unfurled sail of silk. Amid the vessel is a bed on to which the wounded knight sinks in anguish. This is of cypress and white ivory inlaid with gold, the quilt of silk and gold tissue, and the coverlet of sable lined with Alexandrian purple.[1] All this we might regard as merely a poet's fancy were it not that we go on to read that there were set two candlesticks of fine gold with lighted tapers. Here we have the clue. Doubtless the ship, a favourite theme of Christian symbolism, and one which delighted poets and painters and workers in mosaic alike, represented the Church. It is not to be necessarily inferred that Marie, when giving her hero so rare a means of transit, had in her mind all the elaborate symbolism connected with it ; but she had probably read or heard tell of it, and made use of it simply for the enhancement of her story. It is in such ways that we find mysteries embedded, the real significance of them being lost or misunderstood or unheeded, just as the Renaissance painters, without any knowledge of Arabic characters, and solely on account of the ornamental quality of the

---

[1] Compare with this the bed of " King Fisherman " described in *Holy Grail*, vol. i. p. 137, trans. Sebastian Evans, 1898.

lettering, used texts from the Koran, and distorted into mere design the sayings of Mahomet.

In the lay of "The Two Lovers" we again find Christian symbolism in disguise. Here is the old theme of a difficult task to be accomplished by the lover before he can win his lady.[1] The undertaking imposed is the carrying of the loved one to the top of a hill, and our interest in it is enhanced by the fact that the trial was to be made near Pitres, a few miles from Rouen, where there is a green hill, still known as " La Côte des Deux Amans." In Rouen there lived a king who had an only daughter, very fair and beautiful, whose hand was sought in marriage of many. Loath to part with her, he bethought him how he could thwart her suitors. To this end he caused it to be proclaimed far and wide that he would have for son-in-law only him who could carry his daughter to the top of the hill without pausing to rest. Many came, but each in turn failed, greatly to the content of the princess, since secretly she loved, and was loved by, a young knight who frequented her father's Court. At last, constrained by love, the knight, though with much misgiving, determines to undertake the adventure. Before allowing him to do this, the maiden, in order to ensure his success, and herself fasting meanwhile, bids him go to Salerno,[2] near Naples, a school of medicine

[1] Hertz, *op. cit.* p. 396.
[2] This mention of Salerno is of interest on account of the reference to women practising there as medical experts. The origin of the School remains in obscurity, and it is not until the

famous in the Middle Ages, and ask of her kinswoman there, who was well practised in medicine, a draught to give him the needful strength for his task. Returned with this potion, he makes the attempt, but so great is his desire to reach the goal quickly, that he will not slacken his speed to drink from the phial carried by his Love, but hastens forward, only to fall dead as he reaches the summit of the hill.

ninth century, when the names of certain Salerno physicians appear in the archives, that we get any definite information with regard to it. It seems to have been a purely secular institution, but it is quite possible that its development was aided by the Benedictines, who became established there in the seventh century, and who made medical science one of their principal studies. Before the middle of the eleventh century there were many women there who either practised medicine or acted as professors of the science, and some of the latter even combined surgery with medicine in their teaching and treatises. These women doctors were much sought after by the sick, and were much esteemed by their brother-professionals, who cited them as authorities. That the sexes were on an equal footing we infer from the fact that the title of "master" (Magister) was applied to men and women alike, the term "doctor" not having come into use, apparently, before the thirteenth century. Besides the general practitioners and the professors, there were others who fitted themselves specially for military service, as well as priests who added medical knowledge to their holy calling. The teaching followed that of Hippocrates and Galen, and the Salerno school was world-renowned in the art of drug preparation. In the thirteenth century, however, Arab medical writings began to be known in Europe through Latin translations, and Arab practice in medicine, though based on Greek teaching, initiated a new departure. As a result of this, the glory of Salerno waned. Another cause of its decline in fame and popularity was the founding by the Emperor Frederick the Second of a school of medicine at Naples, which he richly endowed, and the rise, un-encumbered by old traditions—for medicine, like scholasticism, could be hampered by dialectical subtlety—of the school of Montpelier.

In this strength-giving potion we may perhaps see the expression of a Christian, and the survival of a pre-Christian belief, where the getting of strength and life is only possible through a direct act of communion, either material or spiritual, with the god. Such world-old beliefs, in which the supernatural intervenes to help the natural, are also intimately connected, even if they are not identical, with the magic of philtres and charms.

We pass from Christian symbolism to magic in the lay of " Yonec." The delightful ease with which mediæval folk turned from magic to religion, or *vice versa*, shows how simply they accepted what they did not understand. At the same time it proves how intermingled the two were, and that what some are inclined to separate now, were once regarded as one and the same thing, the eccentricities and impositions which have developed in both being of mere external growth, and to be treated accordingly. In the lay of " Yonec " a young wife, passing fair, is shut up by her jealous old husband in a great paved chamber in a tower of his castle, to which no one save an ancient dame and a priest has admittance. After seven years of this isolation and uncongenial company, the lady remembers that she has heard tell that means have been found to rescue the unhappy, and she wishes with all her heart that deliverance may come to her. Suddenly a shadow comes across the window, and into her chamber there flies a falcon, which forthwith changes into a knight. As soon as the lady has recovered from her surprise, the knight tells her that he has long loved her, but could not come until she wished for him. Here we have an incident, borrowed direct from Oriental magic, in which a modern believer in psychical phenomena might find an element of telepathy. The will, as in all magic, is the motive power which acts sympathetically on the object of desire, that object being in a receptive condition. Quickly we turn from magic, and the story goes on to tell that the lady, before accepting the knight as her lover, makes it a condition that he believes in God, and the knight offers to prove his belief by taking the Sacrament. This demand is evidently in the nature of a protective test. It was very usual to try some means of discovering whether a person was in league with the powers of evil or not ; for if any one unworthy touched holy things, retribution came at once, either by death or some dire visitation. But how is the priest to administer the Sacrament without seeing the knight ? The latter tells her that he will make himself like her in appearance ; in other words, that he will hypnotise the priest, and make him see what he, the knight, wishes him to. The ruse succeeds, and for a time all goes well ; then comes discovery, despair, and death. The whole story is a most extraordinary medley of fairy-lore, religion, and magic, and most characteristic of the mediæval mind.

MARIE DE FRANCE

The lay of " Eliduc," the last in the manuscript, is also the longest and most elaborate. Marie unfolds her story with so certain yet so subtle a hand, that the reading of it is like the unwinding of some finely illuminated parchment-roll where miniature follows miniature, each perfect in itself, yet all needful to the whole. To the charm of its pictures of mediæval life, with the fine scene between the two women, and their final reunion in the same convent, there is added an incident which gives special interest and importance to the story, since it brings us into touch with one of the oldest and most widespread of traditions—the restoration to life, from apparent death, by means of a flower. There are few pursuits more fascinating than the tracing of traditions, except, it may be, that of symbols, with which they have so much in common. We find the same traditions, just as we find the same symbolic figures, common to the most widely separated peoples, and the real interest in the case of each lies in trying to discover how and why in the course of their migrations their form and their significance have been varied or modified. But before considering the tradition, let us first hear the story.

Eliduc, a knight of Brittany, whose wife, Guildeluëc, was very dear to him, had for over-lord one of the kings of Brittany, with whom, owing to faithful service, he had gained high favour. Being defamed on this account by envious tongues, he was banished from Court, and thereupon determined to quit his country for a while and seek service in the West of England. With many promises to his wife to be faithful to her, he set out for Totnes, where he found many kings ruling in the land, all at war with one another. One of them, a very old man, was ruler in the province of Exeter, and at war with a neighbouring king on account of his refusal to give to the latter his daughter, Guilliadun, in marriage. So Eliduc determined to offer his services to the old king, by whom they were accepted, and by his tact and prowess he soon proved himself worthy of the trust reposed in him. Through a skilful ambush, planned and conducted by him, he defeated the enemy. Guilliadun, hearing of his deeds, sought an interview with him, and at once fell in love with him, and after certain maidenly reserve and hesitation, made her love known to him. This Eliduc secretly returned, but, troubled at the remembrance of his wife and of his pledge to her, his courage failed him to confess that he was already wedded. In order to escape from his dilemma, he sought and obtained the permission of the old king to avail himself of the entreaty of his liege-lord to return to his own country to fight against the enemies who were desolating the kingdom. This permission was granted under his promise to come back if his services were again required. After pledging himself to Guilliadun to do this on such a day

BOAT WITH KNIGHTS AND LADY.

Add. MS. 10294, Brit. Mus.

To face page 49.

as she should name, Eliduc, having exchanged
rings with her, and she having named the day for
his return, departed. Having speedily reduced
the enemies of his liege-lord to submission, he
came once more to England, and immediately
sent to Guilliadun to apprise her of this, and to
beg her to be ready to start on the morrow.
Guilliadun secretly left the castle the next night
and joined her lover, and together they hurried to
Totnes, whence they at once set sail. But as
they were nearing land, a violent storm arose.
Finding that prayers were of no avail, one of
the company cried out, " We shall never make
the land, for you have a lawful wife, and you
are taking with you another woman, setting at
naught God, the law, and uprightness. Let us
cast her into the sea, and anon we shall get to
land." On hearing these words Guilliadun fell
as one dead, whereupon Eliduc in anger struck
the esquire on the head and hurled him into
the sea. When the ship was brought to port
Guilliadun showed no sign of life. So Eliduc,
believing her to be dead, lifted her in his arms,
carried her ashore, and, mounting his horse,
sadly bore her to a small chapel in a forest
adjoining his own lands. Here he laid her in
front of the altar, and covered her with his cloak,
and then returned to his home. Filled with sadness, he arose early each morning and went to
the chapel to pray for her soul, marvelling
nevertheless to find that the face of his Love
suffered no change except to become a little

paler. His wife, made anxious by his melan-
choly and silence, and wondering whither he
went, had him watched, and soon discovered
the truth. Taking a varlet with her, she went
to the chapel, and there discovered the beautiful
maiden, looking like a new-blown rose, and at
once guessed the cause of her husband's sadness
and gloom. As she sat watching and weeping
out of sheer pity, a weasel ran from behind the
altar and passed over the body of Guilliadun,
and the varlet struck it with a stick and killed
it. Then its mate came in and walked round it
several times, and finding that it could not rouse
it, made sign of great sorrow and ran out into
the wood, and returning with a red flower
between its teeth put it into the mouth of its
dead companion, which within an hour came
to life again. Guildeluëc, seeing this, seized the
flower and laid it in the mouth of the maiden,
who after a short time sighed and opened her
eyes. Then she told Guildeluëc that she was
a king's daughter, and had been deceived by a
knight called Eliduc, whom she loved, and who
returned her love, but who had hidden from her
that he was already married. Guildeluëc thereupon made known to her who she was, and sent
at once for her husband. When he came, she
begged him to build a nunnery, and to allow
her to retire from the world, as she would fain
give herself to the service of God. When the
nunnery was ready, Guildeluëc took the veil,
with some thirty nuns, of whom she became the

Superior. Then Eliduc wedded his love, and after some years of happiness they too resolved to retire from the world, Guilliadun joining Guildeluëc, who received her as a sister, and Eliduc going to a monastery which he had founded near by.[1]

In this charming romance, given here in epitome only, the two most interesting points, after noting the mutual suffering of the lovers for love's sake, are the episode of the sacrifice to the sea, and that of the weasel and the life-giving flower. Both these incidents point to the great antiquity of the fundamental theme of the story, which Marie, possibly like many another before her, merely reclothed in garments suited to the fancy of the time. In most stories where the sea has to be appeased by the sacrifice of some one, it is the guilty person who is thrown overboard, or if the offender is not known, lots are cast to determine who shall be the one to make expiation to the god. In the present instance Eliduc is clearly the wrong-doer, but he is the hero, and must be treated as such, and accordingly the hostile voice is the one to be silenced in the depths of the sea.

The other incident—the restoration to life by means of a flower or a herb—frequently occurs

---

[1] M. Gaston Paris (*Poésie du Moyen Age*, vol. ii.), in recalling various legends of "Le Mari aux deux femmes," suggests that the present story, borrowed by Marie from Celtic tradition, is probably of Occidental, and not Oriental, origin, since in the polygamous East the story of two wives would not have furnished a sufficient motive for a special narration.

in classical stories and folk-lore.[1] Perhaps the most familiar example, and, owing to the recent excavations in Crete, the most interesting one, is that connected with Glaucos, son of Minos, king of Crete. In the story (Apollod. iii. 3) Glaucos when a boy fell into a cask of honey and was smothered. His father, ignorant of his fate, consulted the oracle to ascertain what had become of him, and the seer Polyeidos of Argos was named to discover him. When he had found him, Minos shut Polyeidos up in the tomb with the dead body of the boy until he should restore the latter to life. Whilst Polyeidos was watching the body, a serpent suddenly came towards it and touched it. Polyeidos killed the serpent, and immediately a second one came, which, seeing the other one lying dead, disappeared and soon returned with a certain herb in its mouth. This it laid on the mouth of the dead serpent, which immediately came to life again. Polyeidos seized the herb and placed it on the mouth of the dead boy, who was thereupon restored to life.

This story is most graphically depicted on a fifth-century Greek vase in the British Museum, and, whatever its real interpretation may be, it has gained in significance since the life of the distant past of the island has been laid bare, and large jars, which in all probability were used for storing wine and honey and other necessaries, and from their size and contents might well

[1] Warnke, *op. cit.* civ. ; Hertz, *op. cit.* p. 409.

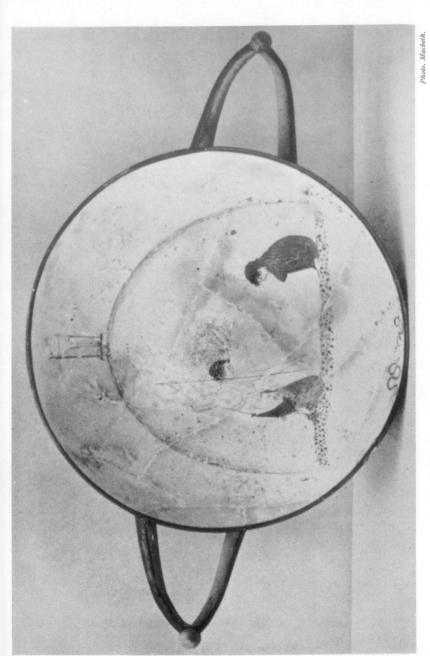

To face page 52.

GLAUKOS AND POLYEIDOS IN TOMB.

Greek Vase, Brit. Mus.

have proved a snare to a venturesome and greedy boy, have been discovered *in situ*. After a lapse of many centuries we find this idea of the life-giving plant reappearing in mediæval garb, daintily fashioned by Marie de France.

Marie, in her story, tells us that the weasel brings a *red* flower. This was possibly the verbena, well known in folk-medicine as vervain, and much used in the Middle Ages. According to one writer, the weasel uses vervain as a preservative against snake-bites, and this idea of its effect might easily have been extended to include death. Even so great an authority as Aristotle mentions that the weasel understood the potent effects of certain herbs. The intervention of a weasel instead of the usual serpent opens up the further interesting question as to whether this weasel incident was not imported from India, where Greek stories had become alloyed with Indian lore. Even to-day, in India, a mongoose, a species of weasel, is sometimes taken on expeditions by any one fearful of snakes, and kept at night in the tent as a protection against them.

In addition to the choice of a weasel as medium, the unusual colour of the flower is also of interest. Giraldus Cambrensis, writing in the twelfth century on the subject of weasels, after remarking that they have more heart than body (*plus cordis habens quam corporis*), goes on to say that they restore their dead by means of a *yellow* flower, and in the still earlier record of the Lydian hero Tylon, where a serpent is the intermediary—and serpents are often credited with a knowledge of life-giving plants,—reference is made to a *golden* flower.[1] This may possibly be connected with the idea of the life-giving power of the god, since the golden flower is dedicated to Zeus. Professor J. G. Frazer thinks that a red flower may perhaps have been chosen to suggest a flow of blood—an infusion of fresh life into the veins of the dead. It is also possible that red and yellow may have been interchangeable terms, just as they are to-day amongst the Italian peasantry. The choice of colour may, however, have been derived from the red anemone, which is said to have sprung from the blood of Adonis, with whom love and life are traditionally associated. There are some, on the other hand, who ascribe to the story a deep spiritual meaning. With them it is not the flower itself which brings about resurrection from apparent death, but the spiritual truth of which the flower is but the outward symbol. It may be that the red blossom represents the joys of earth which Eliduc's wife voluntarily renounces, and which, surrendered to her rival, in time became like a burning thing whose fiery touch awakens to life the sleeping conscience. In a story such as this, which has evidently travelled far and wide before we find it in England in the eleventh century, it is possible that any or all of these surmises may be true.

[1] J. G. Frazer, *Adonis, Attis, Osiris*, p. 98.

MARIE DE FRANCE

The whole of this incident of the weasel and the flower, read in the original, is of extraordinary interest and beauty. What a touching picture of animal sensibility is the account of the despair of the weasel on finding its dead mate, and its tender display of solicitude and sympathy, raising the lifeless head and trying to reanimate the small inert body! Only one who loved animals and knew their habits well could have told thus tenderly and graphically a story so simple, yet so suggestive, of the love of two sentient things, a love which runs like a thread of gold through all creation and makes it one.

The twelfth century was an age of humanism as well as feudalism. As often happens in times of comparative peace, a growth of interest in the individual was springing up and finding expression in lyric poetry and stories. The day of epics was waning. Those vast and involved poems, like to huge and complex frescoes, found little favour at a time when men and women, or at least women, had more leisure and inclination to try to get below the surface of things. Heroes had been glorified till they had almost become deified, and something more personal, more individual, was wanted. By the side of modern romance, where the most sacred and secret intricacies of human nature are, as it were, displayed under the microscope, Marie's narrations may seem somewhat artless. But in putting into words the dawning desires of her time she gave form and impetus to feeling and thought struggling for expression, and gained for her work a definite place in the development of human utterance. Evolution, whether of the spirit or of matter, is the supreme law of things. Marie struck a spark from the ideal which poets and writers down the ages have fanned into a flame.

A THIRTEENTH-CENTURY MYSTIC
AND BEGUINE,
MECHTHILD OF MAGDEBURG

THE triumphant ecclesiasticism of the thirteenth century, manifested in the forms of political power, material wealth, splendid architecture, and worldly positions sufficiently commanding to satisfy even the most ambitious, was, perhaps naturally, accompanied by a gross materialism. Against this the truly pious-minded revolted, thereby causing a reaction towards mysticism. Whilst before the eyes of some there floated, as the ideal, the material ladder leading to fame and power, before those of others there arose, as in a vision, the " Ladder of Perfection," each rung of which gained brought them nearer to the object of their quest—Divine Reality. These latter, whether of great, or lesser, or even of no renown, and amongst whom women played a great and very notable part, were scattered far and wide ; but each one cultivated some little corner of the mystic garden. One such garden was the Cistercian convent of Helfta, near Eisleben, in Saxony, in the thirteenth century a centre of mystic tendencies. It was here that, harassed and ill, Mechthild of Magdeburg took refuge, and entered as a nun in 1270. But we are anticipating.

Mechthild, at first a beguine, and afterwards a nun, but a visionary from the days of her childhood, was born, most probably of noble parents, in the diocese of Magdeburg, in 1212. That she is perhaps better known to the general reader than are other contemplatives of her day is probably due to the suggestion that she may be the Matilda immortalised by Dante in the " Earthly Paradise " (*Purg.* xxviii. 22 *seq.*), rather than to her own writings. This may be partly because the personality of that supreme visionary and poet tended, as does all superlative genius, to cast a shadow over the lesser lights of both earlier and later times, and partly because, although Mechthild's works were early translated into Latin, she wrote in Low German. Though this original MS. has not yet been found, there exists one, translated into High German in 1345 at Basle (a centre of the " Friends of God ") by the Dominican, Heinrich von Nördlingen, by which Mechthild's work has been made known to us, but the language even of this proves a very real stumbling-block to the most strenuous student. Still, by recording her thoughts and visions in the language of her country and her day, she gained a lay audience, a result which would have been hardly possible if she herself had been a classic. But

though no classic—for she says Latin was difficult to her—she evidently, as her work shows,
grew up under the influence of courtly life, and
knew the language of minstrels. She tells us
that her mind was turned to the spiritual life
when she was but twelve years of age, and that
from that time worldly glory and riches became
distasteful to her.   Like the visionary and Saint,
Theresa of Avila, of 300 years later, she took
into her confidence her younger brother, Baldwin,
who later, perhaps under her influence, became
a Dominican.   What we know of her, we know
from her writings, which exist in the above-
mentioned unique MS. (No. 277) now in the
monastery Library of Einsiedeln, a foundation
south of the Lake of Zurich, and still one of the
most famous of pilgrim resorts.   In seeking to
know more of the history of this MS. we get a
most interesting and intimate glimpse of the
methods in religious centres in bygone days,
when MSS. were few.   In quite early times—
how early is not known—there dwelt in the
valleys round about Einsiedeln certain devout
women-recluses, who later lived, as a community,
in four houses, and, ultimately, in a convent.
They were called " Forest Sisters," a name
which may well express the poetry and peace
of their life and surroundings.   Whilst they
were still living in the detached houses, the
MS. was, through Heinrich von Rumerschein of
Basle, sent by Margaret of the Golden Ring, a
beguine of that town, to the one called " The

Front Meadow." Heinrich addresses the gift
"To the Sisters in the Front Meadow." "You
shall know that the book that is sent by her
of the Golden Ring is called *The Light of the
Godhead*, and to this you shall give good heed.
It shall also serve in all the houses of the wood,
and shall never leave the wood, and shall remain
a month in each house. Also it shall go from
one to another as required, and you shall take
special care of it. Pray for me who was your
Confessor, though, alas, unworthy."

In 1235, at the age of twenty-three,
Mechthild—not without many a heart-pang, and
prompted to this determination by a troubled
conscience, a determination doubtless brought
about by the preaching of the Dominican friars,
who were stirring all classes by their impassioned
zeal—left her home and went to Magdeburg,
where she entered a settlement of beguines.
These settlements, semi-monastic in character,
were provided to afford some protection, by
living in community, for women who, whilst
devoting themselves to a religious life, did not
wish to separate themselves wholly from the
world. It was at the time of the Crusades,
when the land teemed with desolate women,
that their numbers increased so greatly, and the
first beguinage was founded about the beginning
of the thirteenth century. The beguine took no
vows, could return to the world and marry if
she so desired, and did not renounce her property. If she was without means, she neither

asked nor accepted alms, but supported herself by manual labour or by teaching the children of burghers, whilst those who were able to do so spent their time in taking care of the sick or in other charitable offices. Each community, with a " Grand-Mistress " at its head, was complete in itself, and regulated its own order of living, though, later, many of them adopted the rule of the Third Order of St. Francis.

Mechthild tells us that she knew but one person in Magdeburg, and that even from this one she kept away for fear lest she might waver in her determination. In this very human way she indicated that her spiritual adventure was no easy matter to her, as, indeed, it could not be so long as her temperament and ideals were at variance. But gradually, she says, she got so much joy from communion with God that she could dispense with the world. As has been well said, " La loi des lois c'est que tout morceau de l'univers venu de Dieu retourne à Dieu et veut retourner à lui."

The book of her writings, which, under divine direction as she opens by saying, she calls *The Flowing Light of the Godhead*,[1] is composed of seven parts, of which six appear to have been written down during the time she was a beguine at Magdeburg, and were collected and arranged by a Dominican friar, Heinrich von

[1] P. Gall. Morel, *Offenbarungen der Schwester Mechthild von Magdeburg, oder das fliessende Licht der Gottheit*, Regensburg, 1869.

Halle, whilst the seventh, consisting of sundry visions and teachings during the last years of her life, was put together just before her death at Helfta in 1282, and, as she pathetically adds, "by strange eyes and hands." In all of these, whilst reflecting in them her inmost feelings, she expresses her entire dependence on spiritual help and inspiration. "The writing of this book," she says, "is seen and heard and felt in every limb. I see it with the eyes of my soul, and hear it with the ears of my eternal spirit, and feel in every part of my body the power of the Holy Ghost."

The general tenor of her writings is contemplative and prophetic. Whilst, as a contemplative, she reminds us of Suso, as a reformer, proclaiming her prophetic warnings, she recalls to us St. Hildegarde, though the latter was a more astute and powerful reasoner. It would seem as if, in general, there are two conflicting tendencies in minds such as Mechthild's, a tendency to tradition—in her case, of course, church tradition—and a tendency to definite self-expression. With Mechthild it was certainly that of self-expression which predominated, for whilst, with her, both co-operated to make a beautiful whole, it was in detail and ornament, so to speak, rather than in the design itself, that she showed her special qualities and gifts. Further, as a mystic, she may be classed with those "for whom mysticism is above all things an intimate and personal relation, the satisfaction of a deep desire," and who therefore fall back "upon imagery drawn largely from the language of earthly passion," as opposed to the mystic whose "longing is to go out from his normal world in search of a lost home, a better country," as well as to the one whose "craving is for inward purity and perfection."[1]

In order to enter into the spirit of her writings, and particularly the prophetic ones, it is necessary to consider how the character and style of her work was induced and affected, on the one hand by her environment and her time, and on the other by her saintly nature and poetic temperament, as well as by her intimate and personal attitude towards things touching the inner life.

The world, in Mechthild's day, was in a state of unrest and of looked-for change. Mankind was ever haunted by forebodings of the approaching happening of something momentous. Whole-hearted faith in the Church was waning, and although outward conformity still prevailed, there existed very diverse opinions, tolerated so long as they did not become too obtrusive. Prophetic writings, giving expression to the yearnings of the time—yearnings fomented and fostered by the prevailing misery caused, in no small degree, by the wars between Pope and Emperor—taught that the world was on the brink of a new era. One of the most influential of these writings, entitled *The Eternal Gospel*,

---

[1] For the suggestive elaboration of this threefold classification, see Evelyn Underhill, *Mysticism*, chap. vi. p. 151 *seq.*

and said to embody the revelations of Abbot
Joachim of Flora (1130–1202), proclaimed that
the dispensations of God the Father and God
the Son—the first two eras of the Church—
were past or passing, and that these would be
succeeded by a third era—that of the Holy
Ghost—when men's eyes would be opened by
the Spirit, and when there would be a time of
perfection and freedom, without the necessity
of disciplinary institutions. In this fair age it
was the hermits, monks, and nuns who, whilst
not superseding the rulers of the Church, were
to lead it into new paths, for to Joachim the
visible Church could not, where all is moving,
remain unchanged, and his counsel was, to keep
pace with the advancing world. Naturally such
sentiments aroused ecclesiastical alarm, and, later,
were condemned by the fourth Lateran Council
(1215), though Dante, withal a good son of the
Church, made bold to see in Paradise the
"Abbott Joachim, endowed with prophetic
Spirit" (*Par.* xii. 140).[1] When Mechthild
wrote her predictions on the last days, Joachim's
teachings, owing to the stir which their un-
orthodoxy had created—not only in the Church
and amongst the preaching friars, but also in the
University of Paris, whence all manner of
polemical discussions freely circulated—were
well known in Germany, and there can be but
little doubt that Mechthild knew of them, prob-

[1] Cf. Edmund G. Gardner, *Joachim of Flora and the Everlasting
Gospel.* Franciscan Essays, Bri. Soc. of Fran. Studies, extra series, vol. i.

ably from the Dominicans, who found special favour in her sight, and that they greatly influenced her own prophetic warnings to the Church.

From these objective conditions which, whilst influencing Mechthild's own thoughts and works, might and did, however differently, influence the work of others as well, we turn to the consideration of her work as the expression of her own poetic soul, welling up from depths filled with love for the highest and most divine things. Before all else we recognise how richly endowed she was with visionary powers and poetic feeling. She revels in beautiful fantasies, as, for instance, when she says, " If I were to speak one little word of the choirs of heaven, it would be no more than the honey that a bee can carry away on its feet from a full-blown flower." With rapture she touches upon the deepest questions of the soul's life, and the highest truths and mysteries of belief, so that in her flights of contemplation her prose becomes poetry, impelled, like some torrent, by the rush of her emotion.

> O thou God, out-pouring in thy gift !
> O thou God, o'erflowing in thy love !
> O thou God, all burning in thy desire !
> O thou God, melting in union with thy body !
> O thou God, reposing on my breast !
> Without Thee, never could I live.

But even so, she does not lose the sense of form or of the picturesque. Some of her writings are clothed in language recalling the Song of Songs, and are, perhaps, echoes of St. Bernard's sermons on that wondrous allegory of the Spiritual Bridegroom and Bride, as when, in a transport, and attempting to express how God comes to the Soul, she exclaims—

> I come to my Beloved
> Like dew upon the flowers.

Others suggest reflections of courtly life and poetry, and at the same time seem to anticipate pictures of the Celestial Garden, bright and blossoming, where Saints tread in measured unison, symbolic of their spiritual felicity and harmony. So with her didactic writings, or with her predictions concerning the decay and corruption in the Church, in which, like some prophet of old, she declaims against such evils in no sparing terms, all alike are fraught with a special grace. In them all the most intimate and the most sublime meet in one expression— the expression of a soul which sees God in all things, and all things in God.

During the thirty years which Mechthild spent as a beguine at Magdeburg, she lived an austere life, and one beset with difficulties, largely created by the fearless way in which she warned and denounced those in high places in the Church. In such denunciations she was not alone, or without good example, for—to name two only of those who stand out pre-eminently on account of their positions and personalities—St. Bernard and St. Hildegarde had both sternly denounced the evils in the Church. "The insolence of the Clergy," says St. Bernard, "troubles the earth, and molests the Church. The Bishops give what is holy to the dogs, and pearls to swine." But the poor beguine, Mechthild, was not in the same powerful position to stay, or even to modify, the resentment which her attacks occasioned. "For more than twenty years was I bound with thee on a hideous gridiron," she writes, likening her anguish to that of St. Lawrence. Nevertheless solace came to her troubled spirit, for, having been warned that it had been said of her writings that they deserved to be burnt, she tells how she prayed to God, as had been her wont when in trouble, and that He told her not to mistrust her powers, since they were from Him, and that no one can burn the Truth.

In many passages Mechthild dwells on the clergy, and her reflections—some very practical, others, to those not versed in symbolism, very quaint—seem to suggest how grievously lacking she considered them to be. Writing in God's name to a canon, she begins by saying that we should, in common with all men, give thanks to our Heavenly Father for the Divine gift which day by day, and without ceasing, pours forth from the Holy Trinity into sinful hearts, and then she quaintly adds, "For that it soars so high, the Eagle owes no thanks to the Owl." Furthermore, she calls upon the priest to pray more, to pay his debts in full, and to live simply, and thus, with humble heart, to set a good example, and, with many other admonitions, she also counsels him to have two rods by his bedside, so that he may chastise himself when he awakes. Mechthild adds that she asked of God how such an one could keep himself without sin in this earthly state, and that God made answer : " He shall keep himself always in fear, like a mouse that sits in a trap and awaits its death. When he eats, he shall be frugal and meek, and when he sleeps, he shall be chaste, and alone with Me."

Touching upon some of the duties of a prior —and here she shows herself eminently practical —she writes : " Thou shalt go every day to the infirmary, and soothe the sick with the solace of God's word, and comfort them bounteously with earthly things, for God is rich beyond all richness. Thou shalt keep the sick cleanly, and be merry with them in a godly manner. Thou shalt also go into the kitchen, and see that the needs of the brethren are well cared for, and that thy parsimony, and the cook's laziness, rob not our Lord of the sweet song of the choir, for never did starving priest sing well. Moreover, a hungry man can do no deep study, and thus must God, through such default, lose the best prayers." From advice to the priesthood, Mechthild turns to warning, and pours forth her reproaches and forebodings with poetic intensity. " Alas, O thou Crown of Holy Christendom, how greatly hast thou lost lustre ! Thy jewels are fallen out, since thou dost outrage and bring dishonour on the holy Christian vows. Thy gold has become tarnished in the morass of unchastity, for thou art become degenerate, and art lacking in true love. Thy abstinence is consumed by the ravenous fire of gluttony, thy humility is drowned in the slough of the flesh, thy word no longer avails against the lies of the world, the flowers of all the virtues have fallen from thee. Alas, O thou Crown of the holy Priesthood, how diminished thou art, and verily thou now possessest naught but priestly power, with the which thou fightest against God and His elect. For this will God humble thee, ere thou learnest wisdom. For thus saith the Lord : ' My shepherds of Jerusalem have become murderers and wolves, for that they slay before My very eyes the white lambs, and the sheep are all sickly for that they may not eat of the wholesome pasture that grows on the high mountains, the which is godly love and holy doctrine.' He who knows not the way that leads to Hell, let him give heed to the unholy clergy, who, with wives and children and many heinous sins, go straightway thither."

Whilst condemning the priesthood, Mechthild eulogises nunnery life in an allegory entitled "The Ghostly Cloister," in which she pictures the virtues as dwelling. "Charity" is the abbess, who with zeal takes care of the congregation in both body and soul ; "Godly Humility" is the chaplain ; "The Holy Peace of God" is the prioress; and "Loving Kindness" is the sub-prioress. "Hope" is the chantress, filled with holy, humble devotion, that the heart's feebleness may sound beautiful in song before God, so that God may love the notes that sing in the heart; "Wisdom" is the schoolmistress, who with all good-will teaches the ignorant, so that the convent is held holy and honoured; "Bounty" is the cellaress; "Mercy" the stewardess; and "Pity" the sick-nurse. The provost, or priest, is "Godly Obedience," to whom all these virtues are subject. "Thus does the convent abide in God, and happy are they who dwell therein."

From this spiritual abode of the virtues we turn to one of Mechthild's earliest recorded visions—that of Hell, with its flame and flare. Whilst Death was perhaps man's first mystery, the Hereafter has been his endless pre-occupation. Whatever his country or his time, he has ever sought to lift the veil which hides the future, portraying his vain efforts in symbol. In Mechthild's time her world was engrossed with thoughts and speculations concerning the Hereafter, for Death, which at the end of the next century was to take dramatic and pictorial form in the weird and all-embracing "Dance of Death," although its earliest known poetic form is of 1160, ever hovered near in pestilence, war, and tumult. Whilst some ex-pressed themselves in carved stone, or on painted wall, others, as did Mechthild, realised their

visions and ideas in a wealth of word-pictures.
Such visions and ideas had accumulated adown
the ages, varying but slightly one from another,
and Mechthild, in making use of this stereotyped
material, only took from, or added to, the general
sum. Yet even so, she contrives to make her
personality felt. She begins : " I have seen a
place whose name is Eternal Hatred." Lucifer,
farthest removed from the source of Light, forms
the foundation-stone, and around him are arranged
the deadly sins. Above him are the Christians,
then the Jews, and, farthest removed from Hell's
dire depths, the Heathen. Horror upon horror
follows, like those pictured a hundred years
before by Herrad von Landsperg, abbess at
Hohenburg, in Alsace, and, fifty years later, by
Dante, and when she concludes by saying that,
after seeing the terrors of Hell, all her five senses
were paralysed for three days, as if struck by
lightning, it is significant that Dante tells that,
overwhelmed with sorrow for the lovers, doomed
for ever to be borne upon the winds, he " fainted
with pity . . . and fell, as a dead body falls."

It is with a sense of relief that we leave such
sad scenes, to glance at her vision of Paradise,
although it does not follow in this sequence in
her recorded revelations, for, as seems fitting, it is
one of the very latest. Calling it " a glimpse of
Paradise," she says that " of the length and breadth
of Paradise there is no end." Then she continues
—and this is especially interesting because it is in
this opening that some commentators have seen

the connecting link with Dante [1]—that between this world and it, she came to a spot—the Earthly Paradise—where she saw trees and fresh grass and no weeds. Some of the trees bore apples, but most of them sweetly scented leaves. Swift streams flowed through it, and warm winds were wafted from the north. The air was sweeter than words can tell. Here, she adds, there were no animals or birds, for God has reserved it for mankind alone, so that he may dwell there undisturbed. This seems to strike a strange note coming from the poetess Mechthild. How different is her sentiment from that of her brother-mystic, St. Francis, to whom the birds were his "little sisters," and who "loved above all other birds a certain little bird which is called the lark." But though, with apparent satisfaction, Mechthild saw no birds, she did see Enoch and Elias, and greeted the former by questioning him as to how he came there. Holy Writ has supplied the only answer, "He walked with God, and he was not, for God took him." Having spoken thus of the Earthly Paradise, Mechthild goes on to tell of the Heavenly, where she sees, "floating in rapture, as the air floats in the sunshine," the souls which, though not deserving of Purgatory, are not yet come into God's kingdom, and to whom rewards and crowns come not until they enter that kingdom. She

---

[1] The tendency of present-day Italian scholarship seems in favour of identifying Mechthild of Hackeborn, rather than Mechthild of Magdeburg, with Dante's Matelda.

then concludes by saying that " all the kingdoms of this world shall perish, and the earthly and the heavenly Paradise shall pass away, and all shall dwell together in God "—the Empyrean of Dante, where he " saw ingathered, bound by love in one volume, the scattered leaves of all the universe ; substance and accidents and their relations, as though together fused, after such fashion that what I tell of is one simple flame."

In her very varied writings many beautiful and suggestive thoughts are to be found, as, for instance, when " Understanding" converses with " Conscience," and accuses Conscience of being at the same time both proud and humble, and Conscience explains that she is proud because she is in touch with God, and humble because she has done so few good works. And again, when " Understanding" and " the Soul" hold converse. Understanding, desirous of knowing everything, asks the Soul why such brilliant light radiates from her, and the Soul replies by inquiring why Understanding asks this, seeing that she is so much wiser than the Soul. When Understanding would still penetrate the unspeakable secrecy between God and the Soul, the Soul refuses to answer, since, as she explains, to her alone is given union with God, to which Understanding can never attain. Or, again, when Mechthild, telling how the Soul, no longer led by the Senses, but leading them to the desired goal, says, " It is a wondrous journey along which the true soul progresses, and leads with it

the senses, as a man with sight leads one who
is blind. On this journey the soul is free and
without sorrow, since it desires naught but to
serve its Lord, who orders all things for the
best."

Of Prayer, which to her was "naught else
but yearning of soul," she says, "It makes a
sour heart sweet, a sad heart merry, a poor
heart rich, a dull heart wise, a timid heart bold,
a weak heart strong, a blind heart seeing, a cold
heart burning. It draws the great God down
into the small heart, it drives the hungry soul
out to the full God, it brings together the two
lovers, God and the soul, into a blissful place,
where they speak much of love."

Again, in a spirit of self-examination, she
writes : "What most of all hinders the
spiritually-minded from full perfection is, that
they pay so little heed to small sins. I tell
you, of a truth, that when I abstain from a
laugh that would hurt no one, or hide some
soreness of heart, or feel a little impatience at
my own pain, my soul becomes so dark, and my
mind so dull, and my heart so cold, that I am
constrained to pray heartily and long, and humbly
to make confession of all my faults. Then grace
comes again to wretched me, and I creep back
like a beaten dog into the kitchen."

But all these and kindred thoughts pale
before her discourses on love. Love was the
keynote of her life. She was born a poetess ;
she became a saint. How sorely she strove

towards this end, and spent herself in conflict between self-control and ecstasy, no words can tell. It was only when Purgation's way was partly trod, and she had "found in Pain the grave but kindly teacher of immortal secrets," that she could say, "Lord, I bring Thee my treasure, which is greater than the mountains, wider than the world, deeper than the sea, higher than the clouds, more beautiful than the sun, more manifold than the stars, and which outweighs all the earth." Then asks the voice of God : "How is this thy treasure called, oh Image of my Divinity ? "

"Lord, it is called my heart's desire. I have withdrawn it from the world, kept it to myself, and denied it to all creatures. Now no longer would I carry it. Lord, where shall I lay it ? "

"Nowhere shalt thou lay thy heart's desire save in My own Divine heart. There only wilt thou find comfort."

Love and knowledge, the two aspirations of the soul after ultimate truth, are her frequent theme. Sometimes she contrasts Love with the knowledge of the understanding : "Those who would know much, and love little, will ever remain at but the beginning of a godly life. So we must have a constant care how we may please God therein. Simple love, with but little knowledge, can do great things " ; sometimes with the knowledge of the heart—"To the wise soul, love without knowledge seems

darkness, knowledge without fruition, the very
pain of Hell. Fruition can be reached only
through Death." In one of her visions she,
in an exquisite simile, describes how love flows
from the Godhead to mankind, penetrating both
body and soul. "It goes without effort," she
says, "as does a bird in the air when it does not
move its wings." In the same vision she sees
the Holy Mother, with uncovered breasts,
standing on God's left hand, and Christ on the
right, showing his still-open wounds, both
pleading for sinful humanity, and she adds that
as long as sin endures on earth, so long will
Christ's wounds remain open and bleeding,
though painless, but that after the Day of
Judgment they will heal, and it will be as though
there was a rose-leaf instead of the wounds.[1]

Of Love, as she conceived it in relation to

[1] The first of these subjects—the Holy Mother and Christ
pleading for sinners—is to be found in a miniature in King Henry
VI.'s Psalter (Brit. Mus. Cotton MS. Domitian. A. xvii. *circ.*
1430, fol. 205), and the two intercessions separately form two of the
subjects in the *Speculum Humanae Salvationis* (fourteenth century).
Though the *S.H.S.* is of later date than the time of Mechthild
the literary source of the subject appears to be a passage in the
De laudibus B.M.V. of Arnaud of Chartres, abbot of Bonneval
1138–1156 (J. Lutz and P. Perdrizet, *Spec. Hum. Sal.* vol. i.,
Mulhouse, 1907), which might quite well have been known to
her, especially if, as Messrs. Lutz and Perdrizet consider, the *S.H.S.*
was written by a Dominican, who would naturally make use of
Dominican teaching and tradition, and we know that Mechthild,
even if not, as has been suggested, a tertiary of that Order, was
in constant and close touch with it. The second subject, the
reference to rose-leaves and Christ's wounds, seems to be a purely
original thought, and one amongst the many fascinating ideas that
have centred round the rose ever since Aphrodite anointed the
dead body of Hector with rose-scented oil (*Iliad*, xxiii. 186).

herself individually, she can never write enough. "I also may not suffer that any single comfort move me, save my love alone. I love my earthly friends in a heavenly fellowship, and I love my enemies with a holy longing for their salvation. God has enough of all good things, save of union with the soul."

But where Mechthild seems to strike an original note for her time is in her insistence on God's craving for the soul, as well as the soul's craving for God. We find the same insistence in Meister Eckhart, who followed her closely in time, and perhaps, in this respect, in thought also. "God needs man," says Eckhart, quite simply. And again, "God can do as little without us as we without Him." With Mechthild it is from ecstasy to ecstasy that "heart speaks to heart." Says the soul of Mechthild : "Lord, Thou art ever sick of love for me, and that hast Thou Thyself well proved. Thou hast written me in the Book of the Godhead. Thou hast fashioned me after Thine own image. Thou hast bound me hand and foot to Thy side. O grant it to me, Beloved, to anoint Thee."

"Where wilt thou get thine ointment, dear one ?"

"Lord, I will tear my happy heart in twain, and lay Thee therein."

"It is the most precious ointment thou couldest give Me, that I should evermore hover in thy soul."

Further God says: "I longed for thee ere

the world was. I long for thee, and thou
longest for me. When two burning desires
come together, then is love perfected."

Sometimes the loving soul traverses a dark
way, and cries out in desolation and despair :
" Lord, since Thou hast taken from me all that
I had of Thee, yet of Thy grace leave me that
gift which every dog has by nature—that in
my distress I may be true to Thee, without any
ill-will. This do I truly desire more than all
Thy heavenly kingdom."

And Divine Love makes answer : " Sweet
Dove, now list to me. Thy secret seeking must
needs find me, thy heart's distress must needs
compel me, thy loving pursuit has so wearied
me, that I long to cool myself in thy pure soul
in the which I am imprisoned. The throbbing
sighs of thy sore heart have driven my justice
from thee. All is right between me and thee.
I cannot be sundered from thee. However far
we are parted, never can we be separated. I
cause thee extreme pain of body. If I gave
myself to thee as oft as thou wouldst, I should
thus deprive myself of the sweet shelter I have
in thee in this world."

Again the soul cries out—but now discomfited
by the Divine Love from whose tireless quest
there is no escape—" Thou hast pursued and
captured and bound me, and hast wounded me
so deeply that never shall I be healed. Thou
hast given me many a hard blow. Tell me,
shall I ever get whole from Thee ? Shall I

not be slain by Thee? Thus would it have been better for me if that I had never known Thee."

Then answers Love : " That I pursued thee gave me delight. That I made thee captive was my desire. That I bound thee was my joy. When I wounded thee, then did I become one with thee. Thus I give thee hard blows so that I may be possessed of thee. I drove Almighty God from His heavenly kingdom, and took from Him His mortal life, and have restored Him with honour to His Father. How canst thou, poor worm, save thyself from me ? "

Of all Mechthild's visions, there is none that seems to reach a greater height of supreme beauty than that in which the loving soul learns the way to its Divine Lover. It is strangely reminiscent of courtly life and courtly poetry, translated into the ecstatic state, and etherealised into the very perfume of spirituality as the soul becomes one with God. Having passed the distress of repentance, the pain of confession, and the labour of penance, and having overcome the love of the World, the tempting of the Devil, and its own self-will, the soul, weary, and longing for her Divine Lover and God, cries out : " Beautiful Youth, I long for thee. Where shall I find thee ? "

Then says the youth : " I hear a voice which speaks somewhat of love. Many days have I wooed her, but never have I heard her voice. Now I am moved. I must go to meet her.

She it is who bears grief and love together. In the morning in the dew is the most intimate rapture which first penetrates the soul."

Then speak her Chamberlains, which are the five senses: "Lady, thou must adorn thyself. We have heard a whisper that the Prince comes to meet thee in the dew, and the sweet song of the birds. Tarry not, Lady."

So she puts on a shift of gentle humility, so humble that nothing could be more so, and over it a white robe of pure chastity, so pure that she cannot endure thoughts, words, or desires which might stain it. Then she wraps herself in a cloak of holy desire, which she has wrought in gold with all the virtues. So she goes into the wood, which is the company of holy people. The sweetest nightingales sing there, day and night, of the right union with God. She tries to join in the festal dance, that is, to imitate the example of the elect. Then comes the youth and says to her: "Thou shalt dance merrily even as my Elect." And she answers: "I cannot dance, Lord, if Thou dost not lead me. If Thou wilt that I leap joyfully, Thou must first Thyself sing. Then will I leap for love, from love to knowledge, from knowledge to fruition, from fruition to beyond all human senses. There will I remain, and circle evermore." [1]

[1] It may be recalled that Dante (*Par.* xxiv.) sees the Saints in Paradise as circling lights from whence issues divine song, and again (*Par.* xxv.) "wheeling round in such guise as their burning love befitted."

Then speaks the youth: "Thy dance of praise is well done. Thou shalt have thy will, for thou art heartily wearied. Come at mid-day to the shady fountain, to the bed of love. There shalt thou be refreshed."

Then, weary of the dance, the soul says to her Chamberlains, the senses: "Withdraw from me, I must go where I may cool myself."

Then say the senses: "Lady, wilt thou be refreshed with the loving tears of St. Mary Magdalene? They may well suffice thee."

"Be silent, sirs; you know not what I mean. Hinder me not. I would drink for a space of the unmingled wine."

"Lady, in the Virgin's chastity the great love is reached."

"That may be. For me it is not the highest."

"Lady, thou mightst cool thyself in the martyrs' blood."

"I have been martyred many a day, so that I have no need to come to that now."

"Lady, bright are the angels, and lovely in love's hue. Wouldst thou cool thyself, be lifted up with them."

"The bliss of the angels brings me love's woe unless I see their Lord, my Bridegroom."

"Lady, if thou comest there, thou wilt be blinded quite, so fiery hot is the Godhead, as thou thyself well knowest, for the fire and the glow which make heaven and all the holy ones burn and shine, all flow from His divine breath, and from His human mouth, through the wisdom of the Holy Ghost. How couldest thou endure it for an hour ? "

And the soul answers : " The fish cannot drown in the water, the bird cannot sink in the air, gold cannot perish in the fire, where it gains its clear and shining worth. God has granted to each creature to cherish its own nature. How can I withstand my nature ? I must go from all things to God, who is my Father by Nature, my Brother through His Humanity, my Bridegroom through Love, and I am His for ever."

Silenced by this wondrous flight of holy passion, we bid farewell to Mechthild. She lived for her time, and she lives for us, as one of " humanity's pioneers on the only road to rest." " Out of the depths," she cried to Heaven. We leave her in the music of the spheres.

A FOURTEENTH-CENTURY
ART-PATRON AND PHILANTHROPIST,
MAHAUT, COUNTESS OF ARTOIS

IT has been well said that "out of things unlikely and remote may be won romance and beauty." Perhaps the truth of this reflection has never been more signally exemplified than in the case of Mahaut, Countess of Artois and Burgundy, the record of whose life, in the absence of any contemporary biographer, has been ably deciphered from such commonplace material as the household accounts of her stewards.[1] This great lady, one of the greatest patrons of art of her time, lived at the end of the thirteenth and the beginning of the fourteenth century. She was a great-niece of St. Louis. No poet has sung of her. It is merely through the prose of daily expenditure that she is made known to us. She stands before us, not the ideal creation of the mediæval romancer, but a real woman, with her virtues and failings, her

---

[1] Richard (Jules Marie), *Une Petite Nièce de S. Louis : Mahaut, Comtesse d'Artois.*

Dehaisnes (M. le Chanoine), *L'Histoire de l'art dans la Flandre, l'Artois, et le Hainaut avant le XVme siècle.*

joys and sorrows, real by very reason of this
union of contrasts, a woman trying to grapple
with difficulties forced upon her by her position,
and by an age when intrigue and cunning were
as freely resorted to, and as deftly handled, as
the sword and the lance.

Mahaut was the daughter of Robert the
Second, Count of Artois, a valiant and chivalrous
man, and of Amicie de Courtenay, of whom it
was said that she was esteemed whilst she lived,
and mourned of all when she died. Her brother,
Philip, predeceased his father, leaving one son,
Robert. In accordance with local custom,
Mahaut, on the death of her father, inherited
Artois, but her nephew, Robert, on attaining
his majority at the age of fourteen, set up a
counter-claim. This family feud was a constant
source of trouble and vexation to her, since
Robert again and again returned to the attack,
not only appealing to the king to consider his
cause, and fabricating spurious documents as a
means of gaining his end, but also employing
unscrupulous agents to spread false charges
against her. He further took advantage of the
growing discontent amongst the nobles, who
were gradually realising that their power was
waning, to attach them to his cause, and to
induce them to join him in harassing Mahaut
by making raids upon her lands and her
castles. She, however, through her extraordinary personality, was able to triumph over
all this opposition, which, far from marring,

only seemed to add lustre to the work she had
set herself to do.

Mahaut was religious, artistic, and literary.
All these characteristics, together with the
circumstance of wealth, she inherited, and right
well did she make use of her inheritance.

Being religious, and living in an age when the
frenzy for crusading had subsided and when architecture was the ruling passion, she expended her
zeal in building religious houses and hospitals.

Being artistic, she made her favourite castle
at Hesdin, and the town around its walls, a
centre of art life. Here, seemingly, she favoured
all the arts, including to a certain extent music,
then still in its infancy, for although she
apparently had no regular minstrel or minstrels
in her employ as was customary in the houses
of the noblesse, she seems to have engaged them
for Church festivals and sundry fêtes, and we
know that on one occasion she hired a minstrel
to soothe her sick child with the sweet soft
music of the harp, thus suggesting that she
herself had felt the power of music to minister
to both body and soul.

Being literary, Mahaut collected what MSS.
and books she could, and the list of them serves
to show what might be found in a library of the
early fourteenth century. Her religious books
included a Bible in French,[1] a Psalter, a Gradual,
various Books of Hours for private devotion,

[1] The Bible was first translated into French, and reduced in size
so that it could be carried in the hand, between 1200 and 1250.

Lives of the Saints and of the Fathers, and the Miracles of Our Lady. Philosophy was represented by a French translation of Boëthius (probably a copy of a translation made by order of King Philip le Bel, by Jean de Meun, the writer of the second portion of *The Romance of the Rose*), Law by a verse translation of the laws of Normandy, History by the Chronicles of the Kings of France, and Travel by *The Romance of the Great Kan*, known to us as *The Travels of Marco Polo*. But by far the largest category consisted of Romances, such as that of Oger le Danois from the national Epic, and another of Tancred, a hero of the first Crusade, the Romance of Troy, Percival le Gallois, Tristan, Renart, and the Violet, the story which forms the chief episode in the play of Cymbeline. Of course there was no great choice, but that Mahaut read them and loved them we may be certain, since we know that she took some with her on her journeyings, and to preserve them from the wear and tear of travel, had leather wallets made to protect them. Mahaut was, in truth, the first wealthy individual of the age to spend her substance with the express purpose of surrounding herself with beauty of every kind. The foremost thought of a man in a like case would probably have been to add to his power. *Her* thought was of beauty, a quality much more far-reaching and less transient, and one which, even like Time itself, triumphs over the changes of fame and fortune.

MAHAUT, COUNTESS OF ARTOIS

Though Mahaut did not live the allotted three score years and ten, she lived long enough to see seven kings on the throne of France, two of whom—Philip the Fifth and Charles the Fourth—were her sons-in-law. She was a mere child when her great-uncle, King Louis, died in 1270. In 1285, the year in which Philip the Fourth, surnamed le Bel, ascended the throne, she wedded Otho, Count Palatine of Burgundy, a widower of forty-five, a companion in arms of her father, and a brave and generous man, who died fighting for his country, but one absolutely incapable in administration, and, as a consequence, always in debt and in the clutches of the usurer. There are few documents to throw any light on her life until after Otho's death in 1303. This may be due partly to the fact that she only came into her great possessions on her father's death in 1302, and partly to the circumstance that the careless and luxurious expenditure of her husband in no small degree dissipated her resources, and naturally prevented, for the time, any material encouragement of art. Doubtless also much of her time was spent in superintending the education of her children—two daughters who were destined to marry kings of France, and a son who was born a peer of the realm, and inheritor of one of its richest territories. But adverse fate, by the disgrace of one of her daughters, and the death of her son, intervened to darken these brilliant prospects, and forms a grey background to her otherwise wonderful and glorious career.

The more the life of this remarkable woman is studied, the more apparent it becomes that what gives it its peculiar charm and worth is the sense she possessed of the value of all human endeavour, whether in great things or in simple. To her the humblest matters of home life, and the affairs connected with the administration of her domains, had each their particular significance. The ordering of a small grooved tablet on which her little boy could arrange the letters of the alphabet claimed her attention equally with the founding and arranging of a hospital. In her capacity as ruler we see the same wide and reasonable outlook on life, for whilst strict as an administrator, in personal relations she was charitable and sympathetic. Sometimes a rebellious baron was deprived of his fief and banished, or was condemned to expiate his misdeed by making a pilgrimage to sundry shrines. But Mahaut was practical withal, and recognised human frailty, and as the pilgrimage was for correction, no pardon was granted unless the offender brought from each of the sanctuaries a certificate that his vow had been fulfilled. On the other hand, if any were sick or in trouble, she was solicitous for their relief, and even aided them personally where possible. She thus put into practice the charge of her saintly kinsman, King Louis the Ninth, who always counselled those about him to have compassion on all mental or physical suffering, since the heart may be stricken as well as the body.

MAHAUT, COUNTESS OF ARTOIS

As Mahaut had no biographer, and contemporary history merely treats her as if she were one of many pawns on a chessboard, her stewards' entries furnish the only materials from which we can weave some outline of her life, an outline, nevertheless, which enables us to reason somewhat concerning her inner life, the pattern, as it were, that is not wrought for the world.

When, in 1302, Mahaut took over the reins of government in Artois, Paris was the great centre of art and literature as well as of the science of the day, a condition largely due to the genius of Philip Augustus, and fostered by succeeding kings. Thither, from far and near, flocked scholars, poets, and artists alike. Some of these took up their abode permanently within its walls. Others passed to and fro, thus creating that constant interchange of thought which is essential to vitality, so that it was said that "the goddess of Wisdom, after having dwelt in Athens and Rome, had taken up her abode in Paris." There, at least twice a year, came Mahaut to her sumptuous dwelling, the Hôtel d'Artois, situated near the Temple, and extending with its gardens and its outbuildings to the walls built by Philip Augustus. Here all who loved the arts and learning were made welcome, and it is interesting to think it possible, nay even probable, that during one of her many sojourns there she may have met and talked with Dante.

Amongst the special treasures to be found

there, mention is made of four figure-pictures, one of which is said to have been of Roman workmanship, and round in form—certainly, as far as is known, a rarity at that time. We also find a record of finely wrought embroideries and tapestries on the walls, and of windows painted either with armorial bearings and figures, or with simple foliage like the delicate ivy and hawthorn to be seen enriching the pages of Books of Hours of the fourteenth century. Special mention is made of a window, evidently over the altar in the private Chapel, in which was represented the Crucifixion. In the large hall were tables on trestles, easily removed before the dance began or minstrels or jugglers displayed their skill, dressers to hold the gold and silver plate and from which to serve the banquet, and settles with footboards so necessary when the rushes were only renewed at lengthy intervals. But if the hall was somewhat sparsely furnished, its ceiling and walls (the latter on occasions hung with embroideries carried from castle to castle as the Countess journeyed) were made bright with colour, and beautiful with design. How bright, and how beautiful, we can infer almost with certainty from examples in the Castle of Chillon of thirteenth and fourteenth century decoration lately rescued from under a coat of whitewash,[1] and from the comparison made by Brunetto Latini (1230–1294), in his *Tesoro*, of the Italian with the French feudal

---

[1] *Chillon*, Albert Naef, Genève, 1908.

castle, in which he says of the one that it is only
built for war, with ditches, palisades, and high
towers and walls, and of the other that it lies in
the midst of meadows and gardens, *with large
painted chambers.*

Mahaut's cousin, the cold and impersonal
Philip le Bel, was on the throne. For the
most part war had ceased in the land, but still
there was war in high places, for Philip,
avaricious by nature, and finding himself a
king under altering conditions — the Papacy
fallen into disregard, the Nobility weakened,
and the Nation growing, but without any adequate
provision made to meet the needs of this growth
—left no stone unturned to supply this want
and gratify his greed. On the question of the
subsidies of the clergy and the relation between
things spiritual and temporal, he quarrelled with
the Pope, Boniface the Eighth, and brought
about the removal of the Holy See from
Rome to Avignon. He robbed and ruined the
Templars, and despoiled the Jews and Lombards,
the financiers of the day. With him no trickery
was too base, no cruelty too cold - blooded.
Gold was his God. Dante, who was his contemporary, refers (*Purg.* vii. 109) to " his wicked
and foul life " (*la vita sua viziata e lorda*), and
(*Par.* xix. 118) to his " debasement of the
coinage " (*falseggiando la moneta*), as well as to
his self-seeking greed. Such, with the added
glamour of art and learning, was the courtly
atmosphere of the Time. The bourgeoisie,

encouraged by the king who sought to aggrand-
ise the monarchy at the expense of the nobles,
was growing rich, and politically gaining in
power, and Philip ere long discovered that he
had helped merely to change the centre of
power, and not to crush it.

But Paris does not seem to have attracted
Mahaut as did her castle at Hesdin. Here she
was in the midst of her own domains, surrounded
by her liegemen and retainers, and able to be in
constant touch with her artificers and workers,
whatever their art or industry. By the thirteenth
century the dwelling of the Noble was no longer
a grim castle, suggestive only of a place of
defence, with narrow slits in the walls for the
admission of air and light and for the discharge
of arrows, but was more like a fortified country-
house. The encompassing walls enclosed a wide
area, within which was sheltered a village and
everything necessary to the growth and development of a community.

From Hesdin Mahaut journeyed constantly
through her County of Artois, visiting her
castles, the towns or villages around them, and
the various religious houses and hospitals she
had founded, and attending in general to the
well-being of her subjects. For her it was not
enough that she was born to reign. She realised
that, without administration, reigning through
the accident of birth is mere puppet's work, and
leads to naught. Her daily life was the visible
expression of this belief, as she herself was an

example of the woman who comprehends the just proportion between personal and public work. That her subjects responded to her sympathy, and held her in affectionate regard, is proved by their kindly and sympathetic concern if she were ill or on a journey, and by the offerings they made to her on special anniversaries and other festive occasions. We read of gifts not only of herrings, sturgeon, game, wine, dogs, peacocks, swans, pasties, and whipped cream, but also of the strangely assorted tribute of a dead bear and twelve cheeses, as well as of one which must have contrasted pleasantly with this sundry and singular good cheer—a parrakeet in a beautifully painted cage. Mahaut, as we have said, was a constant traveller, and though travelling was then no easy matter, the roads could not have been over-much beset with difficulties seeing that she journeyed in all weathers, either on horseback or in a horse-litter, or in a chariot without springs, and with no mean retinue. In truth, her following was like a glorified Canterbury pilgrimage. First came the Countess, accompanied by one or more knights, her ladies-in-waiting, her chaplain and confessor, her physician, her secretary, her treasurer and steward, and sundry petty officers of her household. Then followed the servants, the cook with his scullions, the shoemaker who could also do necessary repairs to the harness, the laundress riding astride as was the manner of serving-women, and a score of lackeys and

dependants of all sorts in charge of the carts
containing the necessaries of travel. These
necessaries were generally packed in wooden
coffers, some of which were simple chests,
whilst others opened like a cupboard and were
fitted with drawers. To preserve such coffers
from damp and damage, they were put into osier
cases covered with cow-hide. And with all this
motley company and baggage, there are but few
records of accidents. The accounts tell of a
small occasional expenditure in consequence of
the breakdown of a chariot, or the fall of a valet
from his horse, or the upsetting into a river of a
cart conveying the Countess's wardrobe. But
such misadventures were not taken very seriously
by these folk, seasoned to discomfort. Valet or
chariot was mended, or the floating garments
were recovered, and on went the easy-going
company, singing by the way, and with horns
blowing as they neared some castle or village
where a halt was to be made for the night.
The absence of any mention of the removal of
furniture from castle to castle during these
periodical wanderings, save a small bed for
Mahaut's own use, leads us to infer that greater
luxury then prevailed than in the days of her
great-uncle, Louis the Ninth, when even Royalty
itself thought it no hardship to have beds and
other necessary pieces of furniture carried by
beasts of burden from place to place according
to the movements of the Court. This frugal
and homely custom on one occasion very nearly

ended in a tragedy. The devout Isabelle, Louis's
sister, was praying in the early morning, as was
her wont, within her curtained bed, and either
lost in prayer or overcome with fatigue by the
length of her orisons, did not notice the arrival
of the packers, who rolled up the bed without
drawing the curtains, and the praying Princess
within must have been smothered had not her
lady-in-waiting, Agnes de Harcourt, heard her
stifled cries, and hastened to her rescue. This
quaint episode so amused Louis, that he ever
after recounted it when telling of the piety of
his sister.

Let us now go in imagination to the Castle
of Hesdin, and see something of its treasures and
of the daily life of the Countess Mahaut.

Soon after her accession to Artois, her two
daughters married sons of King Philip le Bel,
and her little son, Robert, then became her
principal care. A little boy of noble family had
been chosen as his companion to share in his
education and to join with him in play. It would
seem that the two were treated on an absolute
equality, even to having their doublets cut from
the same piece of cloth, and their tunics and
cloaks trimmed with the same fur. Beyond
their ordinary lessons, they were early taught
the games of tables and chess, both of which
were considered essential to a knight's education.
They also rode to the chase and attended tournaments, and at the age of fourteen themselves
held the lance as part of their training in the art

of war. Robert seems to have been of a most inquiring and intelligent nature, but when he had scarce passed his seventeenth year, Mahaut, with scant warning, saw this her only son stricken in death just as he was about to enter the ranks of knighthood. In the archives of Arras, the Capital of Artois, may be found a discoloured parchment containing the inventory of the equipment provided for the youthful Robert in anticipation of his initiation. What sorrow is enshrined in these faded pages ! It is not sorrow for death, but the bitterer sorrow for something that has never lived, or, rather, that has lived only in the heart, like spring blossom blighted ere fruiting-time. In the Church of St. Denis, where modern restoration has but emphasised the transitoriness and vanity of human glory, there can still be seen the tomb of this youth, carved soon after his death by Pepin de Huy, and once painted, as was all such carved work. Even to the mere student it is interesting as being the only existing monument that can with certainty be attributed to this celebrated sculptor, and also as being, in Gothic art, one of the first essays in portraiture in recumbent figures of the dead, as contrasted with mere effigy. For the deeper thinker it has even greater significance. Of all the good and great works that Mahaut conceived and initiated—the churches, castles, hospitals, which she built and enriched for the glory of God and the safety and solace of mankind—all have passed away. This simple tomb alone remains. But its very simplicity is eloquent, for around it there seems to hover that never-dying spirit of love and goodness and beauty to which, throughout her life, Mahaut contributed in such large measure, and which was her real and lasting gift to the world.

Life as mirrored in the Castle records gives little else than a pleasing picture of Mahaut's relations with all her dependants, as well as with those with whom she was connected, whether by ties of friendship, of politics, or of the common courtesies of life. Her immediate household was naturally her first care. Twice a year, at Easter and All Saints, a distribution was made of cloth and furs. Some of these, fine and costly, were for those in personal attendance on the Countess, whilst others were in the nature of liveries. Others, again, of still coarser make, such as Irish serge, with sheep or rabbit skin for warmth in winter, were given to those of lowly service or who had specially rough work to perform. Her ladies-in-waiting, of whom there were always two or three, appear to have received for their services no money payment, but, over and above the cloth and fur already alluded to, gifts, on special occasions, of girdles and satchels (very often jewelled), gold chaplets, and gold and silver braid, jewelled, and used for twining in the hair. In addition to this, presents of jewels and silver cups were made to them by the noble ladies who came to stay with the Countess, just as she, on her part, presented similar gifts to those who accompanied her guests. How well we can picture to ourselves these maidens (for such is all they were), decking themselves in their girdles and jewelled braid, comparing their gifts, and perhaps even standing on some oaken bench the better to get a view of their finery, for the mirrors were small, and the girdles were long, and could not otherwise be seen in all their glory. When they married, the Countess made gifts to them without stint, not only of the beautiful and the needful for their wardrobes, but also of household goods, and sometimes, when she knew their parents or kinsmen to be too poor to provide the usual dowry, even of a sum of money. To the retainers also we find the same kind and helping hand held out. If any were sick they were taken care of, and, if needs be, sent to some place where they could the better be cured, as we read of one who, suffering from gout, was sent to take healing waters. To another retainer was given the necessary money to pay for his son on entering a monastery, another receiving the wherewithal to go to his native village to attend his mother's burial. Old servants, past work, were cared for in the monasteries or hospitals, or given some post suitable to their years. To a poor knight was given money to enable him to buy a good horse and armour, for poverty of purse was no disgrace in the thirteenth century. At the beginning of winter a distribution, organised by the clergy and stewards of the rural communities

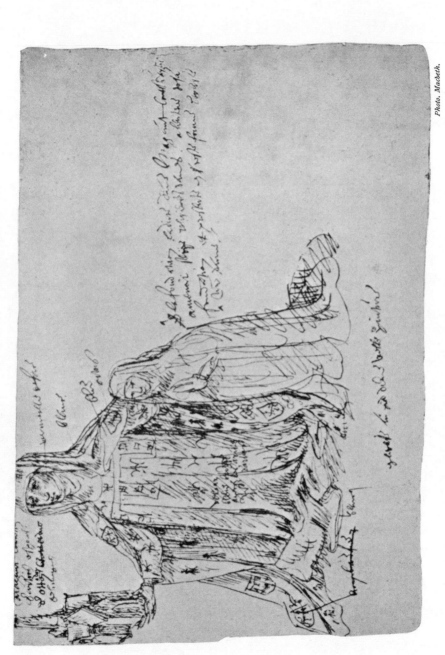

Photo. Macbeth.

STATUE OF MAHAUT IN ABBEY OF LA THIEULOYE, NEAR ARRAS, NOW DESTROYED.

From a Drawing, now in Brussels, made in 1602.

To face page 99.

in Artois, but superintended by the Countess herself, was made to the poor of blankets, garments, and shoes, and so arranged that the same person did not receive the like gift two years in succession. In truth, no details seemed too small, none too onerous, for Mahaut's untiring solicitude. She had heart and brain for everything. It is these intimate touches which make the time so living and present to us, and which seem, as it were, to place this wonderful woman in a charmed and tranquil circle, in spite of the trouble and turmoil incidental to her life and her position.

Amongst Mahaut's many good works was the keeping in repair of existing religious houses, hospitals, and lazar-houses, and the building and maintenance of new ones. Of all the religious houses which she founded, her special care was for the Dominican convent of La Thieuloye, near Arras, the equipment of which, as set out in the accounts, may well serve as an example of that of the others. The items for the furnishing and instalment of the house and chapel include everything needful for the community, from gold and silver vessels, silver-gilt images of St. Louis, the Trinity, and St. John, for the sanctuary, and samite and velvet for chasubles, down to the bowls and platters for the nuns, the woollen material for their garments, and all the simple necessaries of everyday life. In the chapel of this nunnery was preserved a kneeling statue of Mahaut, representing her as foundress,

in the habit of the Order strewn with the arms
of Artois. Jean Aloul, of Tournai, has been
suggested as the sculptor, since it is known
from the accounts that he was working for the
Countess at Arras in 1323. This statue (known
to us through a drawing, now at Brussels, made
in 1602) is of interest to-day because, judging
from the character expressed in the face, it
seems probable that it was a portrait, and not
simply imagery. This conjecture seems all the
more likely when we compare the statue with a
miniature painted more than a hundred years
later by Jean Fouquet in *Les Grandes Chroniques
de France* (Bib. Nat.), portraying the marriage
of King Charles the Fourth with his second
wife, Marie de Luxembourg. In this picture a
lady, heavily coiffed, and with features suggestive
of those of the statue, but with anguish written
upon them, turns away from the ceremony as if
it were all too painful. If this unwilling guest
represents Mahaut, her woeful look is intelligible
when we recall the sad story connected with
Charles's first wife, Mahaut's daughter Blanche,
married when she was but fifteen, and whose
beauty was so dazzling that Froissart records
that "she was one of the most beautiful women
in the world." Accused of an intrigue with a
gentleman of the Court, she was imprisoned in
the Château-Gaillard, where she remained, with
shorn head, until, shortly after Charles ascended
the throne, the Pope declared the marriage null.
Then, whilst the king wedded another, the sad

MARRIAGE OF CHARLES LE BEL AND MARIE OF LUXEMBURG.

Grandes Chrons. de France, Bib. Nat.

To face page 100.

Blanche exchanged her castle prison-house for a
convent one, where she died a year after she had
taken the vows.   There is no reason for suppos-
ing that Mahaut was at the wedding of Blanche's
successor save in the imagination of the artist ;
but for him the inclusion of such a tragic figure
would add a dramatic touch to the representation
of an otherwise conventional ceremony.

It almost takes us aback to read that in
Mahaut's domain of Artois there were at least
eighty hospitals and thirty lazar-houses, without
counting those attached to the monasteries.   But
these numbers will not surprise us so much
when we remember that almost every small
community had its little hospital, used not only
for the sick and as a lying-in hospital, but also
as a shelter for the poor and the pilgrim.   In
the towns they were often built and supported
by the Corporations or by rich merchants.
Evidently some were in the nature of hospitals
for incurables, for there were special clauses
in the deeds of gift providing that a certain
specified number of beds were to be kept for
the sick until they were either cured or released
by death.   Besides building two hospitals in
the County of Burgundy in fulfilment of the
dying wishes of her husband, Mahaut built and
maintained two in her own County of Artois.
The one at Hesdin was the more important,
and we can get some idea of it from the documents of the time.   The deed relating to it
tells that over the large entrance gate there was

carved in stone a figure of St. John, the patron
of hospitals and of the needy generally, with a
poor man and woman on either side of him.
The principal ward was 160 feet long and
34 feet wide, with walls 16 feet high ending in
a gabled roof, with two windows in each gable,
and this, coupled with the fact that the sick
were sometimes laid on cushions by the open
windows, goes to show that what we pride
ourselves on as a special discovery in modern
hygiene—the benefit of fresh air—was known
and applied even in what we are wont to consider a very benighted age in such matters.

Whilst touching upon such a subject as this,
it may be a surprise to some to learn that in
large towns baths were provided for those who
could not afford to have them in their own
homes, and that there were also professional
women hair-washers.

But to return to the hospital. On one side
of the ward were ten windows, each four feet
square, and on the opposite side was a large
door leading into the cloister with its garden,
where the convalescents and the old people,
whilst sheltered, could enjoy the sunshine and
see the flowers and the birds. In addition to
this there was a smaller ward for women, a
chapel, a kitchen, and a room for the matron,
as well as accommodation for the resident doctor,
Maître Robert, and the serving-women. It is
some consolation to think that these poor suffering folk of centuries ago were even thus well

THIRTEENTH-CENTURY TREATISE ON SURGERY, IN FRENCH.

Sloane MS. 1977.

To face page 103.

tended, but when we look at contemporary representations of the surgery of the day,[1] we tremble at the mere thought of the heroic methods adopted. Besides the actual necessaries which she provided for the hospital at Hesdin, Mahaut constantly sent gifts of fish, game, and wine. Similar gifts she likewise made to the hospitals in Artois generally, as well as to those in Paris, and, on fête-days, to the poorer religious houses.

From her beneficence to the sick and sorry, the aged and the poor, we turn to her hospitality to her relations and friends, and to all those in spiritual or temporal authority in the towns or villages of Artois. The Castle of Hesdin, destroyed in the sixteenth century—only a few stones remaining to mark the site,—was situated a few miles from the present modern town of Hesdin. It must have been not only a scene of constant festivity and social intercourse, and a treasure-house withal, but also a veritable hive of industry, with workers and workshops within the Castle enclosure as well as in the town nestling beneath its walls. Here might be found artists and craftsmen of all sorts and degrees—sculptors and workers in stone, ivory-workers, wood-carvers, carpenters, artificers in silver and precious stones as well as in copper, forgers of iron, painters of wall-decoration, stonework, saddle-bows, and even masquerading-

---

[1] See Roger of Parma, *Treatise on Surgery*. French thirteenth century. Brit. Mus., Sloane MS., 1977.

masks, illuminators of MSS., workers and painters of glass, harness-makers, armourers, tailors, and embroiderers—the whole forming a rare and remarkable centre of activity for a woman to have developed and ruled and made into a living force.

It is a fête-day within the Castle. The horns have sounded. The feast is ready. To the great hall repair the knights and the ladies, the esquires and the damsels, two and two, according to their rank, dipping their hands, as they pass in, into silver basins of rose-water. They are gorgeously apparelled in silken garments and cloth of gold and silver, upon which are embroidered their coats of arms, for by the end of the thirteenth century armorial bearings, which by then had become attached to families, were used as a sign of nobility and rank. Mahaut, as hostess, takes her seat last. Adown the table are specimens of silver-plate, some the work of her own craftsmen, others the offerings of friendship or of courtesy. They are fashioned variously, and used for sweetmeats of all kinds, spices, almonds, and dainties made of orange and pomegranate. A favourite form is that of a ship, such as may be seen in *Les Très Riches Heures* of Jean, Duc de Berri, at Chantilly, in a representation of a feast given by the Duke. There are, besides, salt-cellars and sauce-boats, flagons and drinking-cups, and a bowl between every two guests, from which they eat, handing

BANQUET, WITH MINSTRELS PLAYING, AND ROOM HUNG
WITH EMBROIDERY.

MS. Romance of Alexander, 14th century, Bodleian, Oxford.

To face page 104.

Ser y ferret
surtar
Et maintestoie
le escoutar
Se ie ozroie seans mille anne
Le guichet qui estoit de charne

sront reluisant soucez voustie
Lentreoat si nestoit vie vrie
Ametut asse trans y mesine
Le neeent bien fait a droiture
Les voir eut vie come saulsante
Pour faire enuie a toute somme

Photo. Macbeth.

Harl. MS. 4425, Brit. Mus.

To face page 105.

each other dainty morsels. Such, with a knife
and a spoon for each, is their equipment for the
meal, for none, save the carver, has both knife
and fork. In a corner of the hall is a basket
for the broken-meats destined for the poor, a
leathern sack being also provided for foods with
gravy or sauce. Neither at festivals nor in
daily life would a meal have been considered
complete if the poor were not remembered.
Perhaps a messenger arrives during the feast
with the news of a birth or a marriage in
Mahaut's circle of relations or friends, and he
is rewarded with a gift of money, and possibly
receives a silver cup to carry back to the nurse,
or a jewelled chaplet to take to the bride.
Meanwhile the music of trumpets, drums, viols,
and flutes resounds from the minstrels' gallery.
Later, when the feast is ended, and before the
company disperses to walk in the garden if it
is spring or summer, or to look at the beautiful
things in the castle, or to dance or sing or play
chess if it be winter, some one perchance chants
a plaintive ditty to the music of the regal, or
some knight tunes his harp and sings of valiant
deeds, or, may be, of some peerless lady.

But let us look at the rooms of the Castle
and their beautiful contents—the paintings and
embroideries on the walls, the ivories, and the
illuminated Psalters and MSS. And let us go
first into the Countess's own room, which doubtless was near the chapel. We can form some
idea of its decoration and contents from the

accounts, and of its probable arrangement from contemporary plans, illuminated MSS., and pictures. Its walls were adorned with a frieze composed of heads of the kings of France, moulded in plaster and surmounted by crowns of gilded or lacquered tin, below which, on a coloured ground, were fastened fleurs-de-lis, likewise of tin similarly treated. At the end of the room was a bed, a large wooden structure surrounded by a footboard and laced across with cords on which were laid mattresses, a feather bed (sometimes, if we may judge from miniatures, used during the day as a seat on the floor), many cushions, linen or silk sheets, and a fur-lined coverlet. From rods on the ceiling hung curtains which completely enclosed it at night, but which were drawn back and looped up during the day, when the bed was used as a divan. At night a small oil lamp with a float-ing wick was hung within the curtains, and near the bed was a *bénitier*. At the side, separated by a narrow space, there were fixed seats for the accommodation of those who inter-viewed the Countess before she rose. There was a large open fireplace with a bench in front of it which had a movable back, so that the occupant could sit either facing the fire or with his back to it. Close by were wickerwork fire-screens, capable of being raised or lowered at will. Against the walls there were carved chests, enriched with colour, and chairs with leather seats and wickerwork backs, as well as three-legged and folding stools, were placed about the room. At one side of the room was a large oak chair of state with a cushioned seat, and possibly canopied, and close to it a lectern, with hinged candle-brackets, from which Mahaut could the more easily read her MSS., which were often rolled, and difficult to manipulate. In front of this seat was a table, at which any messengers or retainers stood when they sought an interview, or the Countess demanded one. Here also she transacted with her stewards and other agents the business connected with her various castles and her many philanthropic undertakings. Other rooms were painted in plain colour, and hung on special occasions with embroideries and tapestries. Others, again, were decorated with set designs, square or zigzag, in imitation of brickwork, such as may be seen in the Chapel of St. Faith, Westminster Abbey, or with subjects or colour after which they were named. Thus we find mention of the " Parrakeet " room, from the birds painted on the walls, the " Blue " room, from its colour, the rooms of " Roses," of " Vines," and of " Fleurs-de-lis," the room of " Shields," from its frieze of armorial bearings, and that of " Song," from verses traced on the walls, taken from the favourite pastoral of " Robin and Marion," and probably associated with little scenes from the same idyll. The ceilings, with beams and joists painted red, were coloured either green or blue, and strewn with tin stars coated with yellow or white varnish to simulate gold or silver. The lower portions of the walls were often painted in imitation of short curtains, sometimes of but one colour, sometimes gorgeously decorated, but in either case reminiscent of the real draperies hung on festal days. Immediately above there might have been, as in other examples, a border painted with coats of arms, or with a foliated design interspersed with mottoes.

During Mahaut's lifetime this decorative work seems to have been undertaken principally by one special family or community of artists from Boulogne, of which a certain "Jacques" was the leading spirit. In those days artist and craftsman were one and the same. It was the quality, and not the particular subject, of the work that mattered, and thus we find that the painting of a parrot's cage, or of the shafts of a litter, was not considered derogatory for even the most skilled to undertake. From the accounts it would seem that linseed oil was used to mix with the colours, cherry gum or white of egg being added to make them dry more quickly. Payment for work was made three times a year—at Candlemas, Ascension-tide, and All-Saints—or by the day or piece, the last being the form preferred by the business-like Mahaut. Besides such payment, presents were occasionally given for specially fine work, and, if a man was married, a gift to his wife of a gown, or of a cloak with fur, was sometimes added. One of this company of Boulogne artists later on became Court-painter to the Dukes of Burgundy, and took with him not only his trained apprentices from the towns and villages of Artois, and from those bordering on Flanders, but also, doubtless, certain traditions. It is such early migrations of artists, when schools were forming, that have helped to create the difficult problems which confront the student of all early schools of art.

Of embroidery there was such profusion that it is indeed no exaggeration to say that the needle vied with the sword. There were not only wall and bed hangings, embroidered with flowers to brighten winter days, cloaks, gowns, and tunics patterned with gold thread and coloured silks, and beaver hats wrought with gold lace and pearls and sometimes precious stones, but also girdles, satchels, purses, and pennons resplendent with heraldic device, and caparison and harness for the horses. From the East were brought velvets, silks, and stuffs interwoven with gold and silver thread, and used not only for personal adornment, but also for vestments, Church-hangings, and the coverings of litters. As regards tapestry as we understand it—*i.e.* woven in a *high* warp loom—there is apparently no definite mention of its being made at Arras before 1313, so that the numerous allusions to tapestry must refer to stuffs woven in the *low* warp loom. These stuffs would seem to have been of two kinds, the one woven with some simple pattern, the other with heraldic designs of animals or other conventional forms copied from Oriental models. Hence the term " Saracenic " applied to both the workers and their handiwork.

In order to realise the Ivories which were probably to be seen in the Castle of Hesdin, we must go to the Louvre or the British Museum, where may be found a few rare examples of the work of the period, such as caskets carved with scenes from the life of Christ or the Virgin if they were to hold some sacred treasure, or with scenes from some Romance or from daily life if to contain jewels or other mundane objects. In addition to such caskets, often painted, Mahaut had, to hang from her girdle, as was customary with all ladies in the Middle Ages, a daintily wrought ivory writing-tablet, and a small mirror in an ivory case. These mirror-cases were generally carved with a scene from some love-story, such as two lovers playing chess, or going a-hawking, or some detail from the favourite romance of Tristan and Isolde. Possibly amongst these treasures was a saddle-bow, with a wondrous wealth of carving, or chess-men finely modelled, and inlaid with mother-of-pearl, or a triptych with scenes from the Passion, represented under Gothic arches of most superb and delicate workmanship. But it is perhaps in the Chapel that we must seek the finest work, for here both Mahaut and her father, Count Robert, were lavish with unsparing hand. One Jean le

Scelleur, of Paris, a carver of combs and toilet
articles as well as of crucifixes and Virgins, is
named as her principal craftsman. Mention is
made of a Cross carved by him in cedar-wood
with an ivory figure of the Christ, and of two
ivory figures of the Virgin, one under a canopy,
and the other with the Holy Child poised upon
the hip, that sublime motive belonging more
especially to the thirteenth century. The chapel
itself was beautified with carved work in stone.
Over the Altar, and in front of it, were painted
panels, enriched with gold, and translucent
enamel over colour. If we could picture to
ourselves the manner of the sculptor's work we
may recall the " Vine-Capital " in Rheims
Cathedral, where the very stone itself seems
to have been metamorphosed into tender foliage
by the unknown artist.

Of wood-carving, the accounts tell of Choir-
stalls, presses for vestments and various vessels
and ornaments, and also of Angels, gilded and
painted and bearing the emblems of the Passion,
for standing round the High Altar. These are
described as being raised on slender columns,
connected by a bar on which were laced fringed
silk curtains, thus forming a recess for the Altar.
We can get some idea of the simple beauty of
this arrangement from a drawing, still preserved
in the sacristy of Arras Cathedral, of the High
Altar in the old Cathedral, and fortunately made
before the latter, with all its contents, was
destroyed in the sixteenth century. It accords

in every detail with the inventory record of the Chapel of Hesdin. We may also compare a picture (No. 783, "The Exhumation of St. Hubert") in the Flemish room in the National Gallery, where a somewhat similar scheme is shown.

Of the MSS. and Illuminations only brief mention can be made. Surviving examples, and the records of the time, testify to the splendour and the sum of them. At the beginning of the thirteenth century, the French miniature was influenced in no small degree, both in technique and in colour, by glass painting. Towards the end of the century this influence yielded to the prevailing enthusiasm for architecture and sculpture, and in Bibles and Psalters alike there appear scenes with figures as in bas-relief, with architectural backgrounds and decorative details. The same spirit that evolved tender foliage out of the hard stone of cathedral and church evolved also the delicate hawthorn-leaf enriching the initial letter of the MS. It mattered little whether the material worked on was stone or parchment. Each was but a means for giving expression to a newly discovered scheme of beauty—the beauty of Nature. In the thirteenth and fourteenth centuries a renewed impetus had been given to the arts of writing and illumination. This was partly because a demand had arisen for a secular literature to supersede the tiresome and time-worn recitations of minstrels, and partly because, in

the fourteenth century, Books of Hours, instead
of the Psalter alone as had hitherto been customary, came into general use in private devotion.
This created a fresh want, and at the same time
supplied a number of new subjects in which
the artist could reveal his skill. Arras was one
of the chief centres of this new movement,
a movement which Mahaut continued and
stimulated. She employed artists to illuminate
both sacred and secular works for her own use
as well as for gifts—gifts counted beyond
compare and beside which even precious stones
were deemed of less worth. To Mahaut this
desire for beauty was a very lode-star. To
glance at a list of the gold- and silver-smiths'
work—the jewelled and enamelled chaplets of
gold, the jewelled girdles, and buckles, and
braids for the hair, and the cups, some of
silver with crystal covers or wrought with
enamel and precious stones, and others of jasper
mounted with silver work—reads like a fantasy
of hidden treasure in some fairy tale. Even her
chess-boards—and she was a devotee of the
game—were of silver or ivory, and one, we read,
was of jasper and chalcedony mounted with
silver and gems, the chess-men being of jasper
and crystal.

For the younger folk about her there was
tennis, and also games of hazard with forfeits
of girdles and coifs to the ladies. In the Castle
garden were certain mechanical contrivances
which, by their sudden and unexpected action,

were supposed to amuse the unwary guests. One sprinkled them with water, another with black or white powder, as they passed by, and yet another, in the form of a monkey, struck them with a stick, whilst in a bower might be seen a mirror wherein all who looked saw only the distorted semblance of themselves. These unwelcome pleasantries were a part of the miscellaneous borrowings from the East. But for the easily amused folk of the Middle Ages, time passed merrily enough in the midst of such pastimes, and only the shadow on the dial seemed to mark its flight.

But Mahaut, amid the manifold claims on her time and talent, had seen the shadow lengthening. From time to time she had been attacked by illness, to which blood-letting and other remedies of the day had brought relief. But on the 25th November 1329, when in Paris, she was seized with a sudden sickness, so sudden that sinister rumours were noised abroad. Human aid was of no avail. Two days later there was general lamentation. The shadow had lengthened into the night. Mahaut was dead. In accordance with her wishes, she was buried at the foot of her father's grave in the Abbey of Maubuisson, near Paris, her heart being placed in the Church of the Franciscans in Paris, beside the remains of her son, whose tomb there was afterwards removed to St. Denis. Her possession of Artois, for which she had laboured devotedly, became annexed to the Duchy of

Burgundy through the marriage of her grand-daughter with its Duke.

Here, though only a tithe has been told, we must take leave of this cultivated woman of the fourteenth century, a type of the time and for all time. Her aim was the aim of all culture— the attainment of as complete a life as possible. To this she aspired, and to this in large measure she attained. What more can be said of even those we count the greatest?

A FIFTEENTH-CENTURY FEMINISTE, CHRISTINE DE PISAN

CHRISTINE DE PISAN, Italian by birth, French by adoption, may be regarded not merely as a forerunner of true feminism, but also as one of its greatest champions, seeing that in her judgment of the sexes she endeavours to hold the scales evenly. Possessed of profound common sense and of a generous-hearted nature, she is wholly free from that want of fairness in urging woman's claims which is so fatally prejudicial to their just consideration. Although, strictly speaking, Christine was not original, she was representative, and interests us for that very reason. She was perhaps one of the most complete exponents of the finer strain of thought of her time. She stands before us, at the dawn of the fifteenth century, Janus-headed, looking to the past and to the future, a woman typical of a time of transition, on the one hand showing, in her writings, a clinging to old beliefs, and on the other hand asserting, in her contact with real life, independence of thought in the discussion of still unsolved questions.

CHRISTINE DE PISAN

Christine was born at Venice in 1363, where her father, Thomas de Pisan, of Bologna, distinguished for his knowledge of medicine and astrology, had settled on his marriage with a daughter of one of the Councillors of the Republic. When five years of age, she was taken by her mother to Paris to join her father, who had been summoned thither some time before by the King, Charles the Fifth, to serve as his astrologer. At the end of the fourteenth century astrology played a very real and important part in men's lives. Before wars or journeys were undertaken, or additions to castle or chapel made, or even a new garment put on, the stars were consulted for the propitious day and hour. So deeply was Charles the Fifth imbued with a belief in the efficacy of this occult art that when he wished to confer some special honour, or to express his gratitude for some service rendered to him or to the State, he sought to enhance his bounty by sending an astrologer as part of his gift. By the time little Christine arrived in Paris her father had gained the confidence and esteem of the King, and was settled at Court with substantial maintenance. Here she was brought up as a maiden of quality, surrounded by much magnificence, for Charles loved beautiful things, and never stayed his hand to procure them, even when the gratification of his desires involved hardship to his people. He possessed many virtues, but economy was not one of them. The dismal castle of the Louvre,

which had been the home of the French kings
since the days of Philip Augustus, found no
favour in his sight as a place of residence, and
he quickly set about building the sumptuous
Hôtel de St. Paul, in what is now known as the
" Quartier de l'Arsenal." The Louvre he destined
for official functions, for an arsenal, and for his
library. To form a library was no new thing in
Paris. Some thirty years earlier Richard de
Bury, Bishop of Durham (1333) and sometime
Chancellor of England, speaks of his frequent
ambassadorial visits to " Paris, the Paradise of
the World, with its delightful libraries, where
the days seemed ever few, for the greatness
of our love." And he adds, " unfastening our
purse-strings, we scattered money with joyous
heart, and purchased inestimable books." But
whilst it is true that Charles's predecessors had
collected books, none before had thought of
forming a library for public use, and Charles's
work, as M. Delisle remarks, was really the
first germ of the Bibliothèque Nationale.[1]
To collect books was one of his greatest delights,
and he spared no trouble or money to make his
library as complete as possible. This taste for
books he may have inherited from his father,
King John, who, learning to read from a beautiful
Book of Hours, early acquired a love of books
from his mother, Jeanne of Burgundy. Charles
also loved to lend or make presents of books,

[1] L. Delisle, *Recherches sur la libraire de Charles V*, Paris,
1907.

Et commence le liure de la mutacion de fortune.
 omment seur ce possible
A moy simple et pou sensible
De proprement exprimer
Ce quon ne peut extimer
onnement ne bien comprendre

CHRISTINE DE PISAN.

To face page 119.

and among his many gifts, one—an offering to Richard the Second—may be seen in the British Museum (Royal 20, B VI.). The library was considerably depleted during the reign of Charles the Sixth, when it was used as a sort of store-house from which presents were made to prince and prelate, or to any to whom it was desired to make a gift, or a recognition of services rendered. On the death of Charles the Sixth, in 1425, it was bought by the Duke of Bedford, Regent of France, and doubtless some of its treasures were transferred by him into England. Those that were left, and some that gradually found their way back to France, may now be seen in the Bibliothèque Nationale and in other libraries of France, and also in various libraries in other countries, but out of the 1200 books collected by Charles the Fifth, rather less than a hundred are now known to us.

To increase the usefulness of his library, Charles employed a number of translators, not only of Greek and Latin authors, but also of the most important Arabic writings, thus bringing both the classics and the science of the day within the reach of the many students privileged to make use of it. It was in this library that Christine spent long days reading and meditating on the thoughts of the greatest minds, thus fitting herself for the part she had to play when life had ceased to be a gay dream. We can get from a miniature in a Book of Hours, now at Chantilly, and painted by the brothers Limbourg for Jean, Duc de Berri, a brother of the King, some idea of what this old residence of the Louvre was like. In this miniature we see represented a square grim castle, with a large tower at each corner and narrow slits for windows, suggestive more of a place of refuge in time of war and tumult than the home of a peace-loving, enlightened king. When Charles determined to beautify this sombre structure, statues were set up without and tapestries hung within. One of the towers was fitted up for the library, panelled with rare woods and furnished with some thirty small chandeliers and a large central silver lamp, kept lighted both night and day so that work could go on at all hours. In the courtyard an outside circular staircase (one of the earliest, if not *the* earliest, of the kind) was added to give, as was said, a note of gaiety. But the idea of gaiety seems somewhat ironical when we learn that as it was difficult to get a sufficient number of large slabs quarried quickly, headstones from the cemetery of the Holy Innocents were taken for the purpose !

Christine, as a child, showed an extraordinary capacity for learning, and this her father zealously fostered and developed. At the age of fifteen she married, and married for love, the King's notary and secretary, Etienne de Castel, a gentleman of Picardy. Her happiness and well-being seemed assured, but Fortune, whose wheel is ever revolving, though sometimes so slowly as to lull us into forgetfulness, had decreed otherwise. For Christine it revolved all too quickly. Two years after her marriage the King died (1380), and her husband and father lost their appointments. Gradually anxiety and sorrow crept like some baneful atmosphere into the once happy home. First she lost her father, and then, two or three years later, her husband died, leaving her, at the age of twenty-five, with three children to provide for. Like many another, she turned to letters as both a material and a mental support. Endowed with an extraordinary gift of versification, she began by writing short poems, chiefly on the joys and sorrows of love, expressing sometimes her own sentiments, sometimes those of others for whom she wrote. But she tells us that often when she made merry she would fain have wept. How many a one adown the centuries has re-echoed the same sad note !

"Men must work and women must weep." So says the poet. But life shows us that men and women alike must needs do both. And so the sad Christine set to work to fit herself, by the study of the best ancient and modern writers, to produce more serious matter than love-ballads, turning, in her saddest moments, to Boëthius and Dante for inspiration and solace. "I betook myself," she says, "like the child who at first is set to learn its A B C, to ancient histories from the beginning of the world—histories of the Hebrews and the Assyrians, of the Romans, the French, the Bretons, and diverse others—and then to the deductions of such sciences as I had time to give heed to, as well as to a study of the poets." Her master was Aristotle, and she made his ethics her gospel. "Ancelle de science," she calls herself, and remains a humble worshipper at the shrine of knowledge, for knowledge, she says, is "that which can change the mortal into the immortal." We can picture her to ourselves at work in the library of the Louvre, amidst its 900 precious MSS., and in the library of the University of Paris, to which she had access through her friend Gerson, the renowned Chancellor. In a miniature at the beginning of one of her MSS. she is seen seated, in a panelled recess, on a carved wooden bench, dressed in a simple blue gown and a high white coif. She is working at a folio on a large table covered with tapestry, with a greyhound lying at her feet. It is quite possible that this may be either a conventional setting, or one due to the imagination of the artist, but as the miniaturists of those days were, as far as they could be, realists, it is more than possible that we here see her represented at work in her favourite nook in the Louvre library, together with the favourite dog who shared her lonely hours. Gradually solace came to her through work, and having found so precious a treasure for herself, she, like our own modern sage, never tired of preaching to others the gospel of its blessedness.

Whilst Christine wrote and lived her student life—"son cuer hermit dans l'ermitage de

Pensée"—her fame went forth, and princes sought, by tempting offers, to attach her to their courts, but without success. Of these, Henry the Fourth of England, already acquainted with her poems, and Gian Galleazo Visconti, Duke of Milan, were the most importunate, and particularly the former, who was unaccustomed to rebuff and failure. But Christine, with repeated gracious thanks and guarded refusals, remained firm. No reason for her decision is recorded, but it may well be believed that her patriotism would not allow her, even with the certainty of ease and emolument, to quit France at that critical time, or to serve the enemy of her adopted country.

Although Christine's reading was very varied and extensive, there were two subjects—the amelioration of her war-distraught country, then in the throes of the Hundred Years' War, and the championship of the cause of womankind —which specially appealed to her as a patriot and a woman, and for which she strove with unceasing ardour. In all her writings she so interweaves these two causes that it is only by approaching them in the same way that we can understand her view of their psychological unity. To Christine these interests were essentially identical, for she recognised how paramount is woman's influence in the making or marring of the world—how, in truth, in woman's hand lies a key which can unlock a Heaven or a Hell.

There was sore need of a patriot, and in

Christine one was found. It has been well said of her, and by a Frenchman too, that "though born a woman and an Italian, she alone at the Court of France seemed to have manly qualities and French sentiments." France was in a sorry plight. There was war in the land, there was war in the palace. The sick King suffered more and more from attacks of madness, and during these periods the Dukes of Orleans and Burgundy fought for the regency. Christine began her patriotic work by fervent appeals to Isabella, the Queen (to whom she offered a MS. now in the British Museum),[1] to use her influence to put an end to these dissensions which so greatly added to the troubles of the kingdom. She also lost no opportunity of proclaiming in her various writings the duties and responsibilities of kings and nobles to the people, and the necessity, if there was ever to be peace and prosperity, of winning their regard. At the command of Philip le Hardi, Duke of Burgundy, and uncle of the King, she wrote in prose, from chronicles of the time and from information obtained from many connected with the King's household, *Le Livre des faits et bonnes mœurs du roi Charles V*, recounting his virtuous life and deeds and their advantage to the realm, and introducing a remarkable dissertation on the benefit to a country of a strong middle-class. She, of course, reasoned from Aristotle. The subject is a commonplace one now, but in the case of any

[1] Harley, 4431.

one living at the beginning of the fifteenth century, and brought up, as Christine had been, at a magnificent Court, it shows rare independence and breadth of thought to have grasped and proclaimed with such firmness and clearness as is displayed in her treatise the germ of the policy of all modern civilised nations— that a middle-class is essential to bring into touch those placed at the opposite extremes, the rich and the poor.

To Christine belongs an honour beyond that of having been a patriot and a champion of her sex—the honour of having revealed Dante to France.[1] Scattered up and down her writings are many allusions to the *Divina Commedia*, showing how real a place it must have filled in her soul's life. She especially recommends it for profitable study in the place of the " hateful " *Romance of the Rose*, concerning which she gave the warning to her son :—

> Se bien veulx et chastement vivre,
> De la Rose ne lis le livre.

Like Dante, sad and lonely—" souvent seulete et pensive, regretant le temps passé "—like him she also realised the thirst for knowledge as an ever-present want of the soul, and that its ulti- mate perfection is only to be attained by follow- ing after virtue and knowledge. Although, as regards profundity, her conception of the world and of life cannot be compared with that of her

---

[1] A. Farinelli, *Dante e la Francia*, vol. i. p. 192, 1908.

great prototype, or even with that of such an one as St. Hildegarde, still she had read with unflagging diligence a vast number of profane and ecclesiastical writers, and seems to have been well versed in the varied knowledge of her time, especially history. But whilst it is possible to criticise her learning, tempered as this was by her character and the needs of her day, it is at the same time possible to acknowledge that in spite of flaws and an often over-elaborated setting, moral truth sparkles gemlike throughout her writings. One of her biographers speaks of her thus : " Her morale is so pure and so universally human that not only does it remain true to-day, but it will retain imperishable value as long as ever human society is based on a pure and healthy moral foundation."

In her poem *Le Chemin de long Estude*—a title taken from Dante's appeal to Virgil at the opening of the *Inferno*—Christine begins by acknowledging her debt to the immortal poet, saying that much that she has to tell has already been told by " Dante of Florence in his book." Virgil as guide is replaced by the Cumean Sibyl, who appears to Christine in a dream, and offers to conduct her to another and a more perfect world, one where there is no pain and misery. To this Christine consents on condition that " sad Hades, whither Æneas once was taken," is not included in the journey. The Sibyl therefore promises to reveal to her, instead, in what manner misfortune came upon earth, whilst at the same time showing her on the way all that is worth seeing in this world, from the Pillars of Hercules, "the end of the world," to distant Cathay. However exhausting this programme may appear to us, Christine, knowing the real passion of the late Middle Ages for travel—for even those who could not travel in reality did so in imagination,—makes use of it as a setting for the introduction of a discussion on the qualities most necessary to good government. This she does, even at the risk of incurring displeasure in high quarters, recalling how Dante's patriotism led to banishment and death in exile, but she adds, " Qui bien ayme, tout endure." She pours forth her classical examples in a chaotic stream, but when she leaves earth, and ascends to the celestial regions, she not only shows herself versed in the astronomy of the time, but also expresses some beauty of thought. The order of the firmament, where all obey law without ceasing, so that harmony ensues " like sweet melody," reminds her of Pythagoras and Plato, and suggests to her what life on earth might be if good laws were made and observed. In furtherance of her idea, she appeals to Reason, who presides over the Virtues or Divine Powers, to interrogate the three earthly disputants, Nobility, Riches, and Wisdom. In the end Reason awards the prize to Wisdom, condemning Riches as the great enemy of mankind. Thereupon Wisdom appeals to the verdicts of Juvenal, Boëthius, St. Jerome, and others to establish that it is Virtue alone that is of worth, and ennobles a man, and then sets forth the qualities of a good sovereign. But as this leads to some difference of opinion, Christine, who was withal a courtly lady, descends to earth in order to ask the King, Charles the Sixth, to decide the matter. This dream - poem she dedicates to her royal master for his diversion in his saner moments, and thus once again introduces into high places the subject so near to her heart. She lets it be seen that she herself, like Dante, did not believe in the blending of the spiritual and the temporal powers. And as regards temporal power she adds — perhaps borrowing the idea from Dante's *De Monarchia*, and anticipating Napoleon's dream—that in order to ensure peace on earth, it is necessary that one supreme ruler should reign over the whole world. " La sua volontade e nostra pace," sang a soul in Dante's heaven of the Moon—the lowest in the celestial system—when questioned whether it was content with its lowly place. The poet therefore adds, " ogni dove in cielo e paradiso." Christine, echoing these thoughts, would fain apply them to life on earth, giving them their deepest and fullest meaning.

Though she laboured so unceasingly for the good of her country, she also did her utmost to defend her sex from the indiscriminate censure which had been heaped upon it, for the evil spoken seemed to her far to outweigh the good. A century before, Dante had also idealised

woman—even if, as some think, he personified
some abstract quality—and placed her in heaven
beside the Deity. Chivalry had also idealised
woman, but in an exotic, exaggerated manner,
which was bound to reach its zenith, and bound
also to have its darker side. So we find that to
speak good or ill of womankind became a con-
ventionalism in the Middle Ages. Black or
white was the tone chosen by the artist in
words. There was no blending, no shading.
Women were either deified, or held to be evil
incarnate. The material side of life men understood, and could depict with some exactness, but
to grasp in any way its subtler aspects required
an education which could be attained only by
slow degrees, since it meant the gradual modi-
fication of the long-cherished illusion that brute
force is the world's only weapon. A want of
capacity to discern is often responsible for a
depreciatory opinion, and we can but ascribe
this strangely narrow-minded and superficial
attitude towards woman to some such want.
Christine set herself the task of trying to remedy
this evil, not by shouting in the market-place,
but by studying men and women as God made
them and as she found them. Before she began
her work, a new day seemed to be dawning.
Just as, when classicism was in full decadence,
Plutarch wrote *De mulierum virtutibus* (of the
virtue of women), so, in the fourteenth century,
Boccaccio gave to the world *De claris mulieribus*
(of right-renowned women). We do not expect

to find woman treated on a very high plane by Boccaccio, but we recognise that, in a way, this work forms a fresh starting-point in the eternal controversy. Perhaps we should not have had this curious collection of stories of women, virtuous and vicious, mythological and historical —stories which are certainly very inferior as art to those of the *Decameron* — had not a crisis occurred in Boccaccio's life. One day a Carthusian monk came to him with a warning message from the dead, and, much troubled in mind, he resolved to try to begin life afresh. But he was a better story-teller than a moraliser. He would fain save his soul, but he liked and courted popularity, and knew well the deeper meaning of the proverb, "A terreno dolce, vanga di legno." And so he mingles virtue and vice, hoping, as he says, that "some utility and profit shall come of the same." To us of to-day, the chief interest of this work is that Boccaccio's fame perhaps gave a definite impetus to the discussion of the sex, instead of wholesale assertion, and also that it probably suggested to Chaucer the idea for his *Legend of Good Women*. How refreshing to find ourselves in the atmosphere of the kindly Chaucer! Let us pause for a moment, and recall what he says of women, he who was not only a knightly Court‑poet, but also a popular singer, well versed in the practical wisdom of life. In the prologue we read, "Let be the chaf, and wryt wel of the corn," and in allusion to his library of sixty books, old and new, of history and love-stories, he says that for every bad woman, mention was duly made of a hundred good ones. Time and experience in no way dull this appreciation, for when, later, *The Canterbury Tales* appear, his estimate has risen ten-fold, since in the prologue to " The Miller's Tale " we read, " and ever a thousand gode ageyn one badde." From this time onwards, literature on the subject increases almost *ad infinitum*. Treatises and imaginary debates seem to vie with each other for popularity. All these make intensely interesting reading, for these fanciful discussions, which are supposed to take place, sometimes between a man and a woman, sometimes between a mixed company in a garden or villa or some bath resort where many are gathered together, are really a record of the intellectual amusements of the late Middle Ages and the Renaissance. " Que devez-vous préférer, du plaisir qui va vous échapper bientôt, ou d'une espérance toujours vive, quoique toujours trompée ? " " Which sex loves the more easily or can do the better without love ? " "It is not enough to know how to win love, but one must also know how to keep such love when it has been won." Such-like were the subtle problems which on these occasions folk set themselves to solve.

But whilst love problems could be treated as a pastime, they also had their serious side. Of this there is an example in Christine's story of *The Duke of True Lovers*. Although much in its narration is evidently the mere invention of

the poetess, it is quite possible, nay even
probable, that it has some historical basis.
Christine begins her story by saying that it had
been confided to her by a young prince who
did not wish his name to be divulged, and who
desired only to be known as "The Duke of
True Lovers." It has been suggested, with
much likelihood, that this is in truth the love-
story of Jean, Duc de Bourbon, and of Marie,
Duchesse de Berri, daughter of the famous
Jean, Duc de Berri, and the inheritor of his MSS.
When the story opens, the heroine of it, who-
ever she may have been, is already wedded.
Hence all the difficulties of the hero, and indeed
of both. Christine, with her womanly sympathy
and psychological insight, makes all so intensely
real that we are quite carried away in imagination to the courtly life of the fifteenth century.
We read of the first meeting ; of the Duke's
love at first sight ; of Castle daily life ; of a
three days' tournament given in honour of the
lady ; of devices for secret meetings and the
interchange of letters ; of the inevitable scandal-
monger ; of a letter from a former *gouvernante*
—whose aid as go-between had been sought—
containing a most comprehensive and remarkable
treatise on feminine morality, the dangers of
illicit love, and the satisfaction of simple wifely
duty ; of the separation which the position of
the lady, and the gallantry of her lover, alike
demanded ; of meetings at intervals ; of the
mutual solace of short love-poems ; and then

LADY IN HORSE-LITTER, RETURNING FROM TOURNAMENT.

Harl. MS. 4431, Brit. Mus.

To face page 132.

the story, perhaps to evade identification, ends vaguely. But as we finish the story, we cannot help feeling that even if Christine's setting is fiction, she yet gives us a glance of real life.

When Christine turned to her serious work in the cause of womankind, she began by attacking two books, Ovid's *Art of Love*, and *The Romance of the Rose*, both of which, in the Middle Ages, it was deemed wellnigh sacrilegious to decry. Her challenge, *L'Epistre au Dieu d'Amours*, took the form of an address to the God of Love, professing to come from women of all conditions, imploring Cupid's aid against disloyal and deceitful lovers, whose base behaviour she largely attributes to the false teaching of these two books. This argument appeared in 1399, and she soon discovered that she had stirred up a hornet's nest. But she had attacked advisedly and fearlessly, and was quite prepared for any counter onslaught. Her position was considerably strengthened by the alliance and co-operation of her staunch friend Gerson, the Chancellor, who himself, in the name of the clergy, took up arms against the flagrant scurrility to be found in the portion of *The Romance of the Rose* contributed by Jean de Meun. Other powerful allies joined the cause, and, to help to crystallise their efforts, species of "Courts of Love" were instituted, not alone for discourse on love, as heretofore, but also in the defence of women. All who united in this meritorious fellowship undertook to wear a distinctive badge, and thus proclaim their confession of faith. Among these Orders one was styled " L'Escu vert à la dame blanche," another, " L'Ordre de la Rose," and so on, suggestive of their purport. The first-named was founded by the brave soldier Jean le Meingre, Maréchal de Boucicaut, whose portrait may be seen in his superb Book of Hours, painted between 1399 and 1407, now in the Musée Jacquemart-André, Paris.[1] Its membership was restricted to thirteen knights, who swore to defend the honour of women against all detractors. To distinguish them from others less gallantly disposed, they wore on the sleeve an ornament in the shape of a small shield, enamelled green on the outside, and with the representation, on the underside, of a woman, enamelled in white.

> . . . Vous portez la dame en verde targe
> Pour démonstrer que de hardi visage
> Vous vous voulez pour les dames tenir
> Contre ceulz qui leur porteront dommage !

Of the Order of the Rose and its foundation, Christine, in one of her poems, gives most picturesque and interesting particulars, interesting because they are evidently taken from an actual scene, though Christine, in her rôle as poetess, feels it necessary to add touches suggestive of fairyland rather than of real life. A numerous assembly, with goodwill at heart, has met together in the magnificent dwelling

[1] " Le Musée Jacquemart-André," *Gazette des Beaux-Arts*, August 1912.

of Louis, Duke of Orleans, the King's brother,
Christine being one of the number. Suddenly
there comes into their midst one personifying
the Goddess Venus, surrounded by maidens
garlanded with roses and carrying golden bowls
filled with them. The bowls placed on the
table, the Goddess proceeds to announce the
rules of the Order, above all enjoining those
present to avoid envy, and in no way to perjure
themselves, since this would be a most heinous
and hateful sin. The badge chosen is a fresh
rose, but if any member of the Order should
happen to be in a country where such is not
attainable, or when the season is unpropitious,
then a rose fashioned in gold or silver, or one
embroidered in silk, will suffice. With pledges
of loyalty,

> A bonne amour je fais veu et promesse
> Et à la fleur qui est rose clamée,
> A la vaillant de Loyauté deesse,
> Par qui nous est ceste chose informée,
> Qu'à tous jours mais la bonne renommée
> Je garderay de dame en toute chose
> Ne par moy ja femme n'yert diffamée :
> Et pour ce prens je L'Ordre de la Rose,[1]

all the company deck themselves with roses.
The charter is given by the Goddess into the
safe-keeping of Christine, who describes it as
written on fine parchment in letters of azure,
and fastened with a silken cord of the same
colour. From this cord hangs a rare gem, on
one side of which their patroness, the Goddess

---

[1] "Le Dit de la Rose," 197-204, *Œuvres poétiques de Christine
de Pisan*, t. ii., pub. par Maurice Roy, 1891.

of Love, and on the other Cupid, with his feet on a leopard, are depicted. This moral and literary contest is perhaps the most brilliant of the many discussions that took place in the Middle Ages in honour of women. The highest and the wisest in the land joined in it, but all the honour must be given to Christine for having, by her brave and reasonable attitude, caused the problem, which henceforth was to evolve like truth itself, to be treated on a rational basis. "Toute la foy remaint en une femme," says Christine. Were not her words, nearly 500 years later, echoed by Renan when he says, "Après Jésus, c'est Marie de Magdale qui a le plus fait pour la fondation du Christianisme"?

L'Epistre au Dieu d'Amours is an extraordinary product of worldly wisdom and common sense, seasoned with satire. One of the complaints against disloyal suitors, and one which strikes a singularly modern note, is that they make protests of love, and false promises, which must be either paid for dearly, or rejected with scorn. Then the hero, if he has won the day, proclaims his victory in taverns and other places of resort, and even in mixed company. Or if, as is more often the case, he has lost it, he still tries, by suggestive hints, to appear to his fellows a successful gallant. Surely the worldling of to-day does not seem to differ very essentially from his brother of the fifteenth century, or to have progressed any farther along the path of loyalty!

CHRISTINE DE PISAN

Christine's line of argument is that the many must not be condemned for the shortcomings of the few, and that even when God made the angels, some were bad. To the charge that books are full of the condemnation of women, she replies with the simple remark that books were not written by women. Where is the shade of the worthy Christine to-day? Does it walk the earth with a flag of triumph or a laurel wreath whilst its sisters in the flesh are writing on every subject in heaven and earth and sea? "De nos jours, le monde est aux femmes."

Is it marvellous, asks Christine, that a woman—"une chose simplète, une ignorante petite femmellette," as she expresses it—should be betrayed by man, when even the great city of Troy was, and when all the books and romances are full of the betrayal of kings and kingdoms? And if a woman is not constant by nature, why should Jean de Meun, in *The Romance of the Rose*, devise so many tricks to deceive her, seeing that it is not necessary to make a great assault upon a feeble place? Then she deftly turns the tables on the other sex, reminding each that he is the son of his mother, and that

> Se mauvaise est il ne peut valor rien,
> Car nul bon fruit de mal arbre ne vient.

And so on to the end, all is argument and banter. The repute of her letter must have travelled quickly, for whilst Christine was still combating with dissentients, an epitomised rendering of it appeared (1402) in English from the pen of Hoccleve, the pupil of Chaucer, entitled *The Lettre of Cupide, God of Love.*

Later, Christine, with Boccaccio's *De claris mulieribus* before her, writes *La Cité des Dames,* an account of the building of an imaginary city which is to shelter within its strong ramparts the women of all times and all countries who have distinguished themselves by good and heroic deeds. This has been aptly called "The Golden Book of Heroines." It may certainly be considered her masterpiece on her favourite subject. She urges that philosophers and poets, with one accord, have defamed women, and she appeals to God, asking why such a thing should be, seeing that He Himself made them and gave them such inclinations as seemed good to Him, and that in no way could He err. She maintains that God created the soul, and made it as good in woman as in man, and that it is not the sex, but the perfection of virtue, that is material. Combating the suggestion that women are not fit to plead in Court because they have not sufficient intelligence to apply the law when they have learnt it, she refers to history to prove that women who have had the management of affairs have shown that, far from lacking intelligence and judgment, they have possessed both in large measure. At the same time, whilst defending their capability when necessity arises, she does not think it necessary for women

LA CITÉ DES DAMES.

To face page 138.

to interfere in matters which seem essentially man's business. Her remarks on the subject of marriage are certainly practical, and at the same time disclose a strange unloveliness in contemporary manners. She is not of St. Paul's opinion that it is better not to marry, but all the same she suggests that, unless without means, that woman is happier who does not marry a second time, seeing that the life of a married woman is often worse than if she were in the hands of the Saracens—the terror of the Middle Ages,—and that frequently after her husband has been out enjoying himself, her only supper, on his return, is a beating. She counsels the education of women, and condemns those who suggest that this will conduce to unseemly ways. In truth, her wonderful sense of justice, and her enlightened opinions generally, make it a marvellous résumé of statesmanship as far as it goes. It is a real Utopia. Perhaps to Christine it was a glimpse of the Promised Land ! As we read her views on the education of boys and girls together, in this happy city, we feel that she might be discussing with us the problems of to-day. She says that if boys and girls are taught the same subjects, girls can, as a rule, learn just as well, and just as intelligently, as boys, and so on. In this conclusion she forestalls the learned Cornelius Agrippa, a doctor and philosopher of the sixteenth century, and one of the most original and remarkable men of his time, who boldly asserts that sex is merely physical, and does not extend to soul or rational power. She sums up by strongly advocating study and learning, both for self-improvement and as a consolation and possession for all time.

Of her poetical writings on love and the sexes, perhaps the most enchanting is *Le Livre du Dit de Poissy*. In it she takes us, on a bright spring morning, with a joyous company, from Paris to the royal convent of Poissy, where her child is at school. She describes all the beauties of the country, the fields gay with flowers, the warbling of the birds, the shepherdesses with their flocks, the willow-shaded river bank along which they ride, the magic of the forest of St. Germain, a little world apart of greenery and shade, filled with the song of the nightingales. Laughing and singing by the way, they reach the convent gate. Then follows a description of the beautiful carved cloisters, the chapter-house, the nuns' dress and their dormitory, the garden scented with lavender and roses, with one part, where small animals are allowed to run wild, left uncultivated, and the ponds well stocked with fish. As the day wanes, they bid farewell to the nuns, who offer them gifts of purses and girdles embroidered in silk and gold, worked by their own hands. They return to the inn where they are to spend the night, and after supper wander forth to listen to the night-ingales, then dance a carole, and so to bed. The ride back to Paris in the morning, during which a discussion on love matters is introduced,

Cy commence le liure de poissy qui
sadrece abn estrange   xlij
on cliur baillat plain de sauoir
puis qil co plaust a de mee dit auoir
et le mauez p escript fait sauoir
de uostre humblece

SETTING OUT FOR POISSY.

Harl. MS. 4431, Brit. Mus.

To face page 140.

is painted with the same impressionist touch, and it is with real regret that we take leave of these happy folk as they alight in Paris city from their stout nags.

Another similar discourse, *Le Débat de deux amants*, has for setting a gala entertainment, taking place, like the founding of the " Order of the Rose," under the auspices of Louis, Duke of Orleans, who ever extended a princely protection to Christine. Louis had married Valentine Visconti, daughter of Gian Galleazo Visconti, founder of the Certosa, near Pavia, a princess well versed in art and letters, and withal in pomp and splendour. It is on a day in May, the garden gay with gallants and fair ladies. We hear the minstrels play, and watch some of the company, decked with garlands, dancing under the trees. In the palace there is music and singing. Christine is seated in a tapestried hall with one or two esquires who prefer to discourse of love to joining in the jollity. After a time the talk turns on fickle men, and Christine brings forth from her vast storehouse of knowledge classical and mediæval examples. As she mentions Theseus, and recalls his baseness to Ariadne, she points to the tapestry on the wall before them, where the story is woven. This little touch makes the scene very real to us, for the record of the purchase of this tapestry, with the price of twelve hundred francs paid for it, may still be found amongst the royal inventories.

There is such a volume and variety of works

from Christine's pen that it is no easy task to make a fair selection. One of the most significant, since it deals with a subject which permeated mediæval thought, and on which she was wont to dwell, is *La Mutation de fortune*, "Fortune more inconstant than the moon," says Christine. In it she writes with her heart in her hand, as it were, telling first of the sore havoc Fortune has wrought amongst those most dear to her. Yet though her own heart has been torn on the Wheel of Fortune, she stands before her fellow sufferers like some figure of Hope pointing upward, where, she says, wrong is surely righted. And thus she turns to the world in general, not in the spirit of the pessimist, but rather in that of the philosopher. She well knows that Fortune is no blindfolded goddess turning writhing humanity on a wheel, but a something rooted in ourselves, and she has pity for "la povre fragilité humaine." Though so independent and advanced in thought, she is still found clinging in her writings to mediæval forms. As a setting for her thoughts on Fortune's changes, she makes use of the favourite simile of a castle—here the Castle of Fortune—as representing the world, wherein the rich and the poor, the strong and the weak, jostle one another. She criticises all men, from the prince to the pauper, but not women, since these have been sufficiently criticised and decried. It is like the prelude to a *Dance of Death*. Then she tells of the paintings on the walls of this imaginary castle, and uses this mediæval fancy, itself borrowed from the classics (*Met*. ii. 5. 770), to give what is really a history of the world as she knew it, written to demonstrate the instability of all earthly conditions.

Once again, with her versatile gifts, she turns from philosophy to a treatise on military tactics and justice, *Le Livre des faits d'armes et de chevalerie*. However devoid of interest, except as a landmark in the history of military strategy and customs, this work may be to-day, it was thought of sufficient importance in the reign of our Henry the Seventh for the king to command Caxton to translate and print it (1489) with the title of *The Book of Faytes of Arms*, a book still sought after by our bibliophiles. It was further honoured by being quoted as an authority in the reign of Henry the Eighth. Considering the nature of its contents, this seems quite an extraordinary tribute to the judgment and ability of the writer.

But the misery of France is ever increasing. Ceaseless civil war and foreign invasion impoverish the people, and make desolate the land. The dissolute Court is extravagant and filled with discord. Christine, fired with patriotic fervour, once more makes an effort, which proves to be her final one, to arouse the pleasure-loving nobility to some sense of its obligations to the nation. *Le Livre des trois vertues*, and *Le Livre de la paix*, appear one after the other. In the former, which she dedicates to the Dauphine, Margaret of Burgundy, she merely adds another to the long list of discourses for the guidance of women which, in Christian times, begins as early as the second century.[1] This theme forms the subject of so considerable a didactic literature that it can only be hinted at here. Whether treated from a religious or from a social point of view, or the two combined, the sum-total of the teaching is moral training with a view to self-restraint and subordination. Christine addresses herself to all women, from the highest to the lowest, but her principal theme is the influence a princess may and should have on Court life. She further counsels not princesses alone, but all well-born women, not to attach too much importance to the things of this world, to be charitable, and to see to the education of their children, and so to inform themselves that they may be capable of filling their husbands' place when they are obliged to be absent at war or at the Court. She adds a plea for the country, that war should be opposed, and one for the poor, that pity should be shown to them. Then she addresses herself to the towns-woman, advising her to see to her household, not to fear to go into the kitchen, and to avoid all luxury ; then to servants, counselling them on no account to take bribes, adding the practical touch that as God is everywhere, and only asks

[1] A. A. Hentsch, *De la littérature didactique du moyen âge s'adressant spécialement aux femmes*, Cahors, 1903.

of each a good heart, it is not necessary for them to go to Mass every day ; then to the wife of the labourer, bidding her to guard well her master's flocks and to encourage her husband to work ; and, finally, she has a word of sympathy for the poor, holding out to them hope of recompense in heaven for misery endured here, and exhorting them to have patience meanwhile. From this patriotic and practical advice to women she turns to men, and in *Le Livre de la Paix* sets forth the duties of princes and of those in power to the people, importuning them to exercise clemency, liberality, and justice.

But it is too late. The sand in the hour-glass is running low. Disaster follows disaster, until the final blow is struck at Agincourt (1415), where the flower of the French nation is cut off, and princes of the blood are carried away into exile. Christine, with bleeding heart, and worn with trouble and disappointment, retires to the convent of Poissy, " un très doux paradis," perchance to find peace and consolation within its tranquil walls, and to implore Heaven's aid for her sore-stricken country. For fourteen years no sound from her reaches the outside world. Then, inspired by the glorious advent and deeds of Joan of Arc, with all her old passion she pours forth a final hymn of praise and thanksgiving to the woman who has at last aroused France to patriotism, and so dies in peace at the solemn moment of Charles the Seventh's consecration at Rheims.

OF SIX MEDIÆVAL WOMEN

O Thou ! ordainèd Maid of very God !
Joanna ! born in Fortune's golden hour,
On thee the Holy Spirit pours His Flood
And His high grace is given thee for dower.
Now all great gifts are thine :—O blessed be He
That lent thee life !—how word my grateful prayer ?
—No prayer of thine was spoken fruitlessly,
O Maid of God ! O Joan ! O Virgin rare !

. . . .

Mark me this portent ! strange beyond all telling !
How this despoilèd Kingdom stricken lay,
And no man raised his hand to guard his dwelling,
Until a Woman came to show the way.
Until a Woman (since no man dare try)
Rallied the land and bade the traitors fly.
Honour to Womankind ! It needs must be
That God loves Woman, since He fashioned Thee !

. . . .

O strange ! This little maid sixteen years old
On whom no harness weigheth overmuch.
So strong the little hands ! enduring hold
She seemeth fed by that same armour's touch,
Nurtured on iron—as before her vanish
The enemies of her triumphal day ;
And this by many men is witnessèd ;
Yea, many eyes be witness of that fray !

. . . .

Castles and towns, she wins them back for France,
And France is free again, and this her doing !
Never was power given as to her lance !
A thousand swords could do no more pursuing.
Of all staunch men and true she is the Chief,
Captain and Leader, for that she alone
Is braver than Achilles the brave Greek.
All praise be given to God who leadeth Joan !

AGNES SOREL

So much glamour has attached, and rightly so, to Joan of Arc, the soldier-saviour of Charles the Seventh of France, that another woman, Agnes Sorel—Charles's good angel of a less militant order—has been almost entirely overlooked, and where she has been remembered, has been treated by the few with the honour due to her, and by the many merely as Charles's mistress. But to her it was given to be a great inspirer of Charles, and much of the good that this weak king and ungrateful man did for his country may assuredly be in large measure attributed to her influence, just as the greatest merit that can be recorded of him personally was his devotion to her whilst she lived, though the memory of her availed naught after she had passed away. Agnes Sorel came as it were between the ebb and flow of the late Middle Ages and the Renaissance, when chivalry, not as a passing emotion but as an education, still lingered in men's relation with women. Respect for womankind grew in the Middle Ages in France under the double influence of religion and chivalry, of which the cult of the Virgin and the cult of woman were the outcome.

In honour of both, men strove in tournament and fought in battle. With the cry, " For our Lady," or " For God and my Lady," men hurled themselves into the thick of the strife as if the goddess, whether divine or human, in whose name they ventured, had made her champions invulnerable. And, in a manner as it would seem of action and re-action, the goddess became humanised and the woman deified. The former tendency may be traced in miracles attributed to the Virgin, and, later, in the " Mysteries," and the latter in tales of chivalry, where love is treated as a gift from Heaven, and the recipients of it are idealised. Stories which seem to contradict this, and to refute all accepted ideas of chivalry and honour, are frequently original only in details, the bases being borrowed from Oriental tales. Buddha's country, the land of the Zenana, supplied much material of an exaggerated nature which in the West became mere travesty.

It is always difficult to determine exactly the origin of anything so subtle as a sentiment, especially one which gradually pervades and influences a people. It is, in its way, at first like a soft breeze, of which we can only see the effect. But as we try to discover some definite, if only partial, reason for this interchange of simple human relations between the Virgin and her votaries, we remember that St. Francis, the embodiment of exalted human sentiment, had lived, and that scholasticism, in that phase of it which treated the dialectical subtleties of words as paramount, was on the wane. Hence spirit, which had so long been restrained, and which is ever in conflict with form, again prevailed, and mankind discovered that a loving Mother had taken the place of a stately Queen in the Heavens. This attitude towards the Virgin is revealed in the miracles attributed to her agency. It is also shown in one of the greatest works of piety of the thirteenth century, the *Meditations on the Life of Jesus Christ*,[1] which, through the medium of the " Mysteries," introduced into sacred pictorial art some of its most dramatic and appealing scenes. Where is there to be found anything more tenderly human than the incident of " Christ taking leave of His Mother" before His journey to Jerusalem to consummate His mission ?

This note of the womanly element in its fairest form, gradually insinuating itself more and more, and permeating life, art, and literature, is the key to the right understanding of the position which woman had attained in the civilised world.

Before turning our special attention to Agnes Sorel, let us recall the condition of France at the beginning of the fifteenth century.

When the lunatic King Charles the Sixth died in 1422, and Charles, his son, at the age of nineteen, succeeded under the title of " King

---

[1] These meditations, attributed in the past, and by some even now, to St. Bonaventura, are considered by other scholars to be of Cistercian inspiration. P. Perdrizet, *La Vierge de Miséricorde*, 1908, p. 15.

of Bourges," Paris was held by the Burgundians, who were in league with the English. The Dukes of Burgundy and of Brittany were alike vacillating in their policy, being at one time attached to the king's party, and at another allied to the English. With the exception of a few castles, the strongholds of lords loyal to the Crown, the English possessed the whole of France north of the Loire, from the Meuse to the Bay of Mont St. Michel. Hither the Duke of Bedford was sent as regent for the English king, Henry the Sixth, then ten months old, who, by the terms of the Treaty of Troyes (1420), was the lawful king, the right of succession having been conferred on his father, Henry the Fifth, when he married Catherine, the daughter of Charles the Sixth of France.

Charles the Seventh divided his time between Bourges and Poitiers, where the government was carried on, and Loches, Chinon, and Tours, the places he dearly loved, and in which he sought the solitude he craved for. But even in these seemingly peaceful retreats his lethargy and indolence were disturbed by perpetual intrigues, which it must be admitted were largely fostered by his own caprices and fickle affections. Meanwhile a cry of misery was arising from the war-devastated land. Churches and convents, castles and cottages, were all fallen into ruin, and brambles grew on the untilled land where once golden corn had waved. Peasants hid their horses during the day and brought them out to graze at night. As Alain Chartier wrote at the time, "Les pays champestres sont tournez à l'estat de la mer, où chascun a tant de seigneurie comme il a de force." Men of all conditions, from the proudest lord to the poorest peasant, joined in spasmodic and detached efforts to drive out the English, but with the result that they did little else than harass them. Want of cohesion was the characteristic of the national resistance until, from a small village in the east of France, there appeared a deliverer in the person of Joan of Arc. Instantly, as if her sword were a magic wand, all the fighting men, impelled and inspired by the strength of her personality, rallied around her, and victory was assured.

The story of the siege and surrender of Orleans, of the crowning of Charles in Rheims Cathedral, of Joan subsequently falling into the hands of the Burgundians, who sold her to their allies, the English, of her shameful trial and cruel death, are facts so well known that they may well be passed over here as briefly as possible. Suffice it to say, that, except for a time, even the triumph of this maiden-patriot did little to rouse the indolent king, who speedily returned to his selfish life in Touraine. War, pillage, and anarchy again devastated France. But gradually a change came over Charles. He seemed to awake as from a stupor. Dissolute and self-seeking favourites were dismissed, and the king was surrounded by able and high-minded men. He bestirred himself to make a final peace with Burgundy and Brittany, and to take part in the war which was still smouldering, though there were signs of its approaching end.

What was the secret of such a change? That it was due, in the first instance, partly to the wise influence of his mother-in-law, Yolande of Aragon, and partly also to that of his wife, Marie of Anjou, sister of the good Duke René, seems almost certain, but that it was intensified when Agnes Sorel came into his life, there can be no doubt. When we consider the king's earlier life, and what it was whilst he was under the influence of Agnes, and his relapse into indolence and debauchery after her death, we can only attribute much of this change to her sympathetic and wise guidance. Joan of Arc had represented the popular element, Agnes Sorel represented the aristocratic. Joan of Arc aroused the people to united action by her enthusiasm and success, Agnes Sorel, in her time, helped to complete the consolidation of the kingdom, by inspiring and sustaining the king. Perhaps no one man could have accomplished such a revolution. It took two women to do this, and what they did was not of mere passing worth. Phœnix-like, France arose from the ashes of the Hundred Years' War, and it was Agnes Sorel, as priestess, who stirred the embers which hid the new life.

AGNES SOREL

Voltaire, generally more ready to scoff than to approve, wrote thus of Agnes Sorel:

Le bon roi Charles, au printemps de ses jours,

. . . . . .

Avait trouvé, *pour le bien de la France,*
Une beauté, nommée Agnes Sorel.

Was it for the good of France? Let us disregard prejudices, and examine facts. Even then, if all that is known of her were written, it could only bear to this rare personality the resemblance which a faint reflection does to reality.

Agnes Sorel was probably born about 1420 or 1422, in the Castle of Fromenteau in Touraine.[1] Her father, Jean Soreau, or Sorel, was Lord of Coudon, and belonged to the lesser nobility. It was in this beautiful country of forest and meadow-land, of silvery rivers and meandering streams, that Agnes spent her early years, her education being principally religious, for religion naturally held the first place in a society which still retained faith in the supernatural. It was customary at that time for girls of noble birth to complete their education either at Court or at the castle of some princely person, for such places were considered excellent schools of courtesy and other virtues for the daughters as well as for the sons of the nobility.

---

[1] Both the date and the place of her birth seem uncertain. Some writers suggest 1415, and some 1420 or 1422, as the date; whilst Froidmantel, in Picardy, is conjectured by some, and Fromenteau, in Touraine, by others, as the place. (Du Fresne de Beaucourt, *Hist. de Charles VII*, t. iv. p. 171, note 4.)

Though the date is uncertain, it was at the Court of Lorraine that Agnes became maid-of-honour to the Duchess Isabelle, wife of René, Duke of Anjou and Lorraine, and Count of Provence, a prince distinguished for chivalry and learning. This intellectual and chivalrous atmosphere must have been peculiarly congenial to the sympathetic and versatile nature of Agnes Sorel. We can picture her listening to the Duke René reading his latest poem to one or two of his brother-poets in the castle pleasaunce, or discoursing on philosophy or statecraft, or attending some brilliant pageant or sumptuous fête. Chivalry, though dead as an institution, still survived as a recreation, and as an appeal from the past to the cultured imagination, and René, mediæval knight that he was in sentiment, dearly loved the gorgeous spectacle of a tournament, with the knight jousting in honour of his chosen lady. At this Court Agnes also came under the influence of Yolande of Aragon, widow of Louis, King of Naples and Sicily, great-granddaughter of King John of France, mother of the Duke René, and mother-in-law of King Charles the Seventh, a woman renowned for her extraordinary political capacity. All these ties, and the remembrance of the French blood in her veins, emphasised Yolande's dominant passion—the love of France,—and it may well be that in this patriotic atmosphere Agnes Sorel became imbued with a like passion, which later she was to develop in all its perfection,

rivalled only by her devotion to the well-being
and glory of her royal lover.

Patriotism was a virtue of recent growth in
France, for, in order to thrive, it requires unity
of idea, and during the Middle Ages the only
idea common to all was Christianity, which,
from the nature of its teaching of humility and
fraternity, does not make for patriotism. It
may cement the structure, but it does not form
the basis. It was only after years of suffering
and unrest that men learned to sink their
individual and local interests in those of the
nation as a whole. Then, and only then, could
patriotism arise, and only under such conditions
could it flourish.

How long Agnes lived at the Court of
Lorraine (one of the most refined and cultured
Courts of the time), and how her first meeting
with the king came about, is uncertain. It has
been considered likely that between 1431 and 1435
Isabelle of Lorraine went to Chinon to beseech
the king to use his influence to obtain the release
of her husband, imprisoned by his cousin, a rival
claimant to the duchy of Lorraine. It is possible
that Agnes, even if only born in 1422, may have
accompanied her, but even if she did not, this
visit of Isabelle's may, indirectly, have led to
the meeting between the king and Agnes.
Whilst still a prisoner, René succeeded to the
crown of Naples on the death of his brother,
Louis d'Anjou, and as the country was in a
disturbed condition it was deemed prudent for

Isabelle, his wife, to act as his substitute, and, as *lieutenante générale*, she set forth to establish his claim. History is silent on the point as to whether Agnes accompanied her or not. It may be, as some seem to think, that she remained in Anjou with Isabelle's eldest daughter, Marguerite, afterwards Queen of England. We should like to think that it was during this time that she attracted the notice of Charles, for this would lend additional interest to the exquisite miniature in the Musée du Louvre (at one time in the Book of Hours of Etienne Chevalier, now for the most part at Chantilly), which it seems probable represents Agnes Sorel as a youthful shepherdess, with the Castle of Loches in the background and Charles the Seventh riding towards her. As we have already suggested elsewhere,[1] this may have been a poetical rendering of their first meeting. However this may be, it seems probable that it was soon after the year 1435[2] that she first attracted the notice of Charles, and that, later, she took up her residence in Touraine, no doubt gaining her influence over the king at first by her beauty, which all her contemporaries proclaim, and afterwards by that mysterious combination of ability and grace, of intelligence and physical vitality, which held him captive for many years. During this time she, like a true woman, and no ordinary place-

---

[1] *Athenæum*, June 25, 1904.
[2] Du Fresne de Beaucourt, *Hist. de Charles VII*, t. iii. p. 286.

hunter, made his devotion to her react upon himself, for the good of his country and to his own honour. She not only counselled him wisely herself, but persuaded him to surround himself with wise counsellors.

Of these counsellors, and the able and devoted men who served the king in divers ways, some few stand out more prominently than the rest, because of their position of intimacy in the royal circle, and their special and enduring friendship with Agnes Sorel. Such were Etienne Chevalier, Treasurer of France; Pierre de Brézé, of a noble Angevin family, and Sénéchal of Normandy after the expulsion of the English; and Jacques Cœur, the king's superintendent of Finance, whose house at Bourges, with its angelceiled chapel, still delights the traveller.

Etienne Chevalier was for some time secretary to the king, and after filling one or two smaller posts connected with finance, was made Treasurer of France, and member of the Grand Council. In addition to administrative capacity, he possessed a brilliant intellect and a great love of art. It is to his initiative that we owe the only suggestions in portraiture of Agnes Sorel. It was to him also that the king confided the supervision of the erection of the monuments to her memory at Jumièges and Loches—Jumièges where she died in 1449, and where her heart was buried, and Loches her favourite place of sojourn, and to whose church and chapter she had made large gifts. To Loches her body was

borne in royal splendour, and there laid to rest
in the choir of the church in a simple tomb.
We can imagine the loving care with which
Etienne Chevalier watched the sculptor, and
possibly even gave him suggestions, as he
fashioned in alabaster her recumbent effigy
representing her with hands clasped as if in
prayer, her feet resting against two lambs, and
her head guarded by two angels with outstretched wings. Perhaps this stone effigy was
the one true portrait of Agnes, but the head and
face were partially destroyed during the Revolution, and restored in their present form in 1806,
so that little of the original now remains.

This tomb, which to-day may be seen in a
small vestibule of the Château Royale (now the
Sous-Préfecture), has a strange and chequered
history. Perhaps scarce another has suffered
such singular vicissitudes, so many removals, or
more ruthless violations. Soon after the death
of Charles the Seventh (1461), the canons of
Loches, whom Agnes had largely endowed and
of whom she asked naught save to be remembered in their prayers, petitioned Louis the
Eleventh for its transfer to a side chapel, since
they considered it unfitting for the dust of such
an one to repose in the choir. Louis, using his
subtlety to better purpose than was his wont,
replied that if they removed the tomb, they
must return her gifts. Naturally these worthy
ecclesiastics silenced their consciences and kept
the tomb where it was. However, in the year

TOMB OF AGNES SOREL.

AGNES SOREL

1777, in the reign of Louis the Sixteenth, the priestly conscience again awoke to the enormity of its presence within the choir, and, with the king's consent, it was removed to the nave. Before re-burial the coffin was opened in the presence of various church dignitaries and State officials. Among the latter was a doctor who left an authoritative account of the proceedings, from which we can approximately surmise the height of La Dame de Beauté, and verify the record of her abundant fair hair. The exterior coffin of oak was only 5 feet 6 inches long. Within this, and protected by another of lead, was a shell of cedar wood in which, after the lapse of more than three centuries, lay all that was mortal of Agnes Sorel. Her fair hair was plaited in a long tress, and two curls rested on her forehead. As one of those present, more curious than his fellows, stretched out his hand to touch, all fell to dust. Death and Time were her guardian angels. But even this desecration did not suffice to drain the cup of unmerited vengeance. In 1793 the tomb was rifled, the sculptured features, so lovingly wrought, defaced, and her dust cast to the winds. But what matter? Agnes had done her work— work which had to be done, and which she alone could do.

Another of the little band of chosen spirits of which Agnes was the soul and centre, was Pierre de Brézé, Lord of Varenne and Brissac, who early showed himself a man of affairs, and was admitted to the King's Council when he was but twenty-seven. In war, administration, and finance, he proved himself equally trustworthy and skilful, and to these qualities he added others of a brilliant intellectual nature. He advanced from one post of trust to another, until the king himself presented him with the keys of the city and castle of Rouen. Thus he became Sénéchal of Normandy, an honour which remained in his family. One of his grandsons, Louis de Brézé, a son of Charlotte, daughter of Agnes Sorel and Charles the Seventh, was the husband of Diane de Poitiers.

Jacques Cœur, whose life was so intimately associated with the Court during Agnes's lifetime, and so sadly marred and ended after her death, was the son of a simple merchant of Bourges. Following in the wake of many adventurous and ambitious merchants of the time, he journeyed to the East and amassed a large fortune, which he placed at the disposal of the king. This enabled Charles to carry on the war in spite of his impoverished exchequer, and to make a final and successful effort against the English. But, like many another on whom Fortune has smiled, evil tongues and envious hearts began, ere long, their vampire work, and after the death of his friend and patroness, Agnes Sorel, Charles made no effort on his behalf, but left him at the mercy of his calumniators in the same base and heartless way in which he had abandoned Joan of Arc. Jacques, his goods confiscated, and his life in danger, was obliged to fly the country, and died fighting, in the Pope's service, against the Turk.

Of the beauty of Agnes Sorel there can be no doubt, for all contemporary chroniclers and poets tell of it. Even the Pope, Pius the Second, allowed himself to add his tribute of praise to the general homage. Considering that there are so many types of physical beauty, appealing to as many different temperaments, there must have been something rare and remarkable in Agnes to have attracted and held bound all who came in contact with her. We can but conclude that this unanimous judgment could only have been the result of that mysterious union, so illusive, so indefinable, of spiritual with physical beauty. The records of the time merely tell us that she had blue eyes, and fair hair in abundance. The only picture, and this not done from life, by which we can judge her—for the miniatures by Fouquet, at Chantilly, from Etienne Chevalier's Book of Hours, though exquisite in delicacy, are too minute for much characterisation—is, even if we accept it as the original from Fouquet's hand, an overcleaned work in the Museum at Antwerp.[1] This, or the original painting, formed a wing of the so-called diptych painted to adorn the tomb of Etienne Chevalier and his wife in the Cathedral of Melun, the other wing—now in the Royal Museum, Berlin

---

[1] Du Fresne de Beaucourt, *Hist. de Charles VII*, t. iv. p. 171, note 2.

—representing Etienne Chevalier himself, in the attitude of prayer, his patron saint, St. Stephen, beside him. There seems reason, however, to suppose that this offering of Etienne's was in fact a triptych, and that the missing wing pictured his young wife, then lately dead (1452). If this was so, Etienne and his wife would have appeared in adoration on either side of the Queen of Heaven, here personated by Agnes Sorel, thus bringing the panel with Etienne's portrait into harmony with the central panel, which otherwise it fails to be.

Of the miniatures at Chantilly, the whole series of which forms a most tender and rare tribute to wife and friend, only brief mention can here be made of those concerning Agnes. The most simple and beautiful in sentiment and design is that of the *Annunciation*, in which the seated Virgin, in the likeness of Agnes Sorel, with bowed head receives the angel's message. The scene is laid in a Gothic chapel (perhaps the Sainte Chapelle with slight adaptations to suit the artist's fancy),[1] with statues of the Prophets all around, and Moses, holding the Books of the Law, as the central figure of the group. This assemblage of Old Testament seers certainly typified the Old dispensation, whilst the Annunciation prefigures the New, and to us the whole may not unfitly form an allegory of the new order which Agnes Sorel was to help to bring about. In another minia-

[1] Cf. *Grandes Chroniques de France*, fol. 292, Bib. Nat.

BOOK OF HOURS OF ETIENNE CHEVALIER.

To face page 162.

BOOK OF HOURS OF ETIENNE CHEVALIER.

To face page 163.

ture—the *Visit of the Magi*—Charles the Seventh, accompanied by his Scottish guard, and with the Castle of Loches in the background, himself kneels as one of the kings before the Virgin, here also represented in the likeness of Agnes. And so on, throughout the series, in many of the scenes of the Virgin's life we find her bearing the features of Agnes until an older and sadder type becomes necessary in the *Crucifixion*, the *Entombment*, and the *Announcement of the Death* and the *Death* of the Virgin. When, however, death has transfigured age and sorrow, the likeness of Agnes reappears in the *Assumption*, and *Coronation*, and, the crowning glory, the *Enthronement* of the Virgin.

In a Book of Hours, at Munich, painted about 1500 A.D. for Jacques Cœur's grandson (in part perhaps by Jean Bourdichon, the artist of the superb Book of Hours of Anne de Bretagne now in the Bibliothèque Nationale, or at least by some pupil or follower of his), there are three miniatures that seem of special interest in connection with Agnes Sorel. One is a representation of the Virgin of the Annunciation, and another that of the Madonna with the Holy Child. In both these the features of the Virgin Mother appear to faintly echo those of Agnes as we know her, as the crowned and ermined queen in the picture at Antwerp. Still more interesting is the third miniature, giving a view—here used as a setting for the *Procession to Calvary*— of the front of Jacques Cœur's stately dwelling at Bourges. Here doubtless many a time Agnes and the king were entertained. Hither Jacques returned from sundry journeys to the East, laden with treasures to beautify his surroundings. Hence he fled, the victim of success. Over the principal entrance is a canopied recess, once sheltering an equestrian statue destroyed during the Revolution. This now empty space once held a statue of King Charles the Seventh, armed cap-à-pie on a galloping caparisoned charger, as he may be seen represented on medals of the period. It is not a little significant of this thankless monarch that he here seems to be turning his back on the house of his faithful servant and supporter, and to be riding away. Other details worthy of mention in this Book of Hours are the realistic background to the picture of the *Visit of the Magi*, with its snow-covered village church, houses, and fields ; the Italian drug-pot in the Magdalen's hands in the scene of the Crucifixion, showing the intimate intercourse with Italy ; and the Mater Dolorosa seated *alone* at the foot of the Cross,—a tragic note taken from the *Mystery of the Passion*.

There is only one unanimous opinion concerning Agnes Sorel, and that is as to her beauty. For the rest, it would seem as if prejudice and flattery held the scales. The mean is difficult to discover, and perhaps it is only possible to get somewhere near it by studying results—the remarkable change, as already noticed, in Charles's life and conduct whilst under her influence.

AGNES SOREL

In the face of conflicting records it is no easy matter to determine when Agnes Sorel first became the king's mistress. In 1435, when the Treaty of Arras was concluded between Charles and the Duke of Burgundy, Cardinal de Sainte-Croix (afterwards Pope Pius the Second) was Papal legate at the French Court, and aided in the negotiations. He tells in his memoirs that the relation between Charles and Agnes was known publicly at the time, and that the king could do nothing without her, even having her at his side at the royal councils. The trustworthiness of this statement has, however, been so questioned, that it seems safer to endeavour to arrive at the truth from other sources, although, if the statement can be relied on, it seems to follow, almost as a matter of course, that Agnes must have been born earlier than 1422. It is an admitted fact that between 1433 and 1438 the manner of Charles's life entirely changed. In the year 1433 the infamous and once all-powerful favourite, La Tremoille, who had been the king's evil genius for six years, and was largely responsible for the king's treatment of his wife, Marie of Anjou, was dismissed at the instance of the politic Yolande. Yet even so, the king often relapsed into indolence and apparent indifference to his kingly duties, and it was not till after 1438, when he summoned a national Council at Bourges, that Charles showed himself to be a new man. It is also not long after this that we read of favours granted by the king to Agnes's relations. From that time, Charles ceased to spend his time in dreamland, as it were, in the sweet Touraine country, and engaged himself in affairs of State, listening to and accepting wise counsels, favouring the restoration of schools and universities—which, in the uncertain state of the country, had almost ceased to exist—and encouraging the final efforts to expel the national enemy, even at times personally joining in the fight. If we see in this, in a measure at all events, the guiding spirit of Agnes, the secret of her influence is not very difficult to discover. Apart from her beauty, which, with Charles, would be a potent factor, Agnes had a woman's insight and skill in her relation with him, ever holding up to him the glory and obligations of kingship, at the same time herself entering, with all the vitality of her extraordinary nature, into his favourite pastimes. We know that in one or other of her many residences near Chinon or Loches, she and the king often spent the evening playing piquet or chess (the latter being his favourite game), and then, on the morrow, rode forth together to the chase. So the days were passed in work and simple outdoor pleasures, Agnes taking no recognised public part in the king's life, but devoting herself heart and soul to the task she had in hand. But besides these relaxations of peace, there was also the reality of war ; for the war still lingered on, though feebly. The English had lost their ally, the Duke of

Burgundy, as well as Bedford, the able Regent, and there was no fit man to take the latter's place. Paris opened her gates to Charles in 1436, and in the following year Charles, after having reigned for fourteen years, made his first State entry into the capital of his kingdom, mounted on a white charger, the sign of sovereignty. In 1444 a treaty was concluded at Tours with the English, and, to make the compact doubly sure, Margaret of Anjou, a niece of the king, was married to Henry the Sixth of England. For about a month the Court and its princely visitors gave themselves up to fêtes and pageants, and it was during this time of rejoicing that the position of Agnes was officially recognised. She was made lady-in-waiting to the queen, and took a prominent part throughout the festival. Charles gave her the royal castle of Beauté, on the Marne, near the Bois de Vincennes, "le plus bel chastel et joly et le mieux assis qui fust en l'Isle de France," desiring, as was said, that she should be "Dame de Beauté de nom comme de fait." From the time of her public recognition she appeared with the king at all the brilliant festivities celebrated in honour of treaties and marriages. She also sat in the royal council, a position which, as a king's mistress, she was the first to occupy, though we know that Henri II. took no step without first conferring with Diane de Poitiers, and that Madame de Maintenon sat in Louis the Fourteenth's privy council.

OF SIX MEDIÆVAL WOMEN

The change which came over France after the Treaty of Tours was marvellous, alike in its extent and its rapidity. Commerce was again resumed between the two nations; men and women once again ventured without the city walls, to breathe, as it were, the fresh air of liberty; and those who had been called upon to fight, returned to their work in the fields or the towns. We cannot better voice the feeling of the people than by borrowing the song of a poet of the day:

> Le temps a laissé son manteau
> De vent, de froidure et de pluie,
> Et s'est vêtu de broderie,
> De soleil rayant, clair et beau;
> Il n'y a beste ne oiseau
> Qu'en son jargon ne chante ou crie:
> Le temps a laissé son manteau.

Now that Agnes had assumed a definite rôle at Court, she lived principally at Loches, where the king assigned to her "son quartier de maison" within the castle, and also gave her a residence without the walls. Here she shone like a radiant star; for although the king did not have much personal influence on the movement in art and letters, his Court was the meeting-place of many distinguished and intellectual men. Among them we find the name of Alain Chartier, the poet, and sometime secretary to the king, and one of the ambassadors who went to Edinburgh to ask the hand of the little Margaret of Scotland for the Dauphin. We remember him now chiefly in connection with the charming story told of this girl-wife of the Dauphin Louis. Betrothed to Louis when she was a child of three, and sent to France to be brought up at the Court, she was married at twelve to this boy of thirteen, who could not possibly appreciate her simple, sweet nature which endeared her to all others. One day as she was passing with her ladies through a room in the castle, she saw Alain Chartier lying on a bench asleep. She approached quietly, and kissed him, much to the surprise of her attendants that she should " kiss so ugly a man." And she made answer : " I did not kiss the man, but the precious mouth whence so many beautiful and fair words have issued." Poor little poetess ! Fortunately her life was a short one. She died when she was just twenty-one, with these words on her lips : " Fi de la vie de ce monde, ne m'en parlez plus." The scientific historian of to-day is inclined to dismiss this story as a pleasing though rather foolish romance. But even so, Alain Chartier may be remembered as a poet and philosopher, as well as a brave and wise patriot during some of France's darkest hours—a worthy contemporary of Agnes Sorel and Joan of Arc. Fearing neither the nobles nor the people, he blames the former for their love of luxury and personal indulgence, and exhorts both to think of the public good, and to aid in their country's defence, instead of allowing themselves to be engrossed with their private affairs. Then, whilst acknowledging that as he has not the strength to bear arms, it is only with his pen and his speech that he can serve his country, he reminds them that it was the historian's pen and the orator's harangue, just as much as the warrior's lance, that made the glory of the Romans.

Louis the Dauphin, come to man's estate, and self-seeking and treacherous, was no friend to Agnes, who had incurred his hatred by her fearless disclosure to the king from time to time of conspiracies against his person, in which Louis was the prime mover. After repeated reconciliations, the king in despair finally banished him to his domain of Dauphiné. The traitor, quitting the royal presence for what he deemed exile, swore to be avenged on those who had driven him forth, and if some of the records of the time speak truly, four years later his opportunity came, and he kept his oath.

The last scene of Agnes's life was pathetically interesting. Her end came almost suddenly. The king, listening to advice, had resolved to continue the war in Normandy,[1] and, at the instigation of Agnes, if we may believe the words of a courtly writer of the time, had himself gone to the front. Rouen was taken, and Charles entered in triumph. The streets were decked with flowers and branches, and the houses hung with rich draperies, and everywhere

---

[1] Lavisse, *Hist. de France*, vol. iv. part 2, p. 229, footnote.

the leopards and quarterings of England had been replaced by the fleur - de - lis. Charles, preceded by a gorgeous procession of archers, each company arrayed in the livery of its lord, and carrying his special banner, followed, under a canopy, on a horse caparisoned to the ground with blue cloth sprinkled with fleurs-de-lis of gold, surrounded by princes and the principal captains and officers of the Crown. With his wonted observance of religious duty, slowly he made his way to the cathedral through the shouting multitude, and to the sound of many fiddles and the fanfare of trumpets. There he descended, kissed the relics as he knelt beneath the great portal, and then entered its hushed and solemn dimness to return thanks. But scarce had the air ceased to ring with the plaudits of the people, when the report of a plot against the king, devised by the Dauphin, is said to have come to the ears of Agnes, and she hastened to the king at Jumièges, whither he had retired for a short rest during the unusual and inclement winter. Here, stricken by a mysterious sickness, by some thought to be typhoid fever, by others attributed to poison administered at the instigation of Louis, she died in February 1450, in her manor of Mesnil, near the Abbey of Jumièges. The king was with her to the end, and could only be induced to withdraw when her lifeless form sank back in his arms. So died this wonderful and fascinating woman who had lived and laboured for her country through perhaps the most critical period of its history.

It is impossible to entirely ignore what has been written to Agnes's personal discredit, though much of it may well be looked upon as exaggeration, and open to suspicion. That the king was not her only lover may be true, but in the absence of satisfactory documentary evidence of this, perhaps the various intrigues attributed to her may, for the most part at least, be regarded as the creations of scandal. Still, bearing in mind the condition of France at the time of her accession to power, the extent of the influence she admittedly exercised in the councils of the king, and the great change which came over the royal fortunes and the fortunes of the country during the years of her ascendancy, it is scarcely possible to refuse to her some right to share in the recognition so lavishly bestowed upon the other great woman of that time—Joan of Arc. The one may be said to have been the complement of the other. Both were necessary to the needs of the day, and the glory of successful accomplishment should be shared between them.

A NOTE ON MEDIÆVAL GARDENS

MEDIÆVAL GARDENS [1]

No one can study French mediæval lore, or
Gothic cathedral, or Book of Hours, without
realising how great a love of Nature prevailed
in the late Middle Ages. The poems tell of
spring, " the season of delight," of gardens which
suffice " for loss of Paradise," and of birds " with
soft melodious chant." In the dim stillness of
the cathedral, Nature is expressed in infinite
variety. Foliage grows in the hollows of the
mouldings, and sometimes, as at Chartres, even
the shafts, as they tower into the gloom, end in
half-opened leaves, suggestive of spring, of hope,
and of aspiration. Many a sunny façade shows
us scenes of rural life—sowing, reaping, vine-
dressing, and so forth—fashioned as a calendar
in stone, and many a peasant must have rejoiced
as he saw himself and his occupation thus
represented in effigy. Fortunately for the poor
toiler, the Church not only taught that " to
labour is to worship," but further honoured
work by thus representing it at the very entrance

[1] The quotations from the *Roman de la Rose* are taken from
Mr. F. S. Ellis's translation, published by Messrs. J. M. Dent & Co.
in the " Temple Classics."

to the sanctuary, so making it, as it were, the
" open sesame " to higher things.

In Books of Hours and illuminated MSS.,
before the complete border of flowers, birds, and
small grotesques was developed, we find ornamental flourishes, like the growth of ivy and
hawthorn, splendidly free in design, and painted
with evident joy even in the minutest bud or
tendril. Everywhere may this love of Nature
striving for expression be seen. But we must
turn to the poems and romances if we would
fully realise it in all its simplicity and truth,
since it is in these alone that we get at the
actual mediæval feeling unalloyed with all that
we ourselves have, perhaps unwittingly, read
into it.

" All hearts are uplifted and made glad in the
time of April and May, when once again the
meadows and the pastures become green." So
says one of the old romancers. And this joy
in returning spring seems to have pervaded
mediæval thought and expression. Little is
this to be wondered at when we call to mind the
long dreary winters spent in cold and ill-lit
castles, or in dark, draughty houses and hovels.
Before glass, long regarded as a luxury, came into
general use in dwellings, the only protection
from rain and cold consisted in wooden shutters,
or movable frames with horn slabs (necessarily
small), or varnished parchment. In truth, the
only warm, bright place was the chimney
corner, and here, as near as might be to the

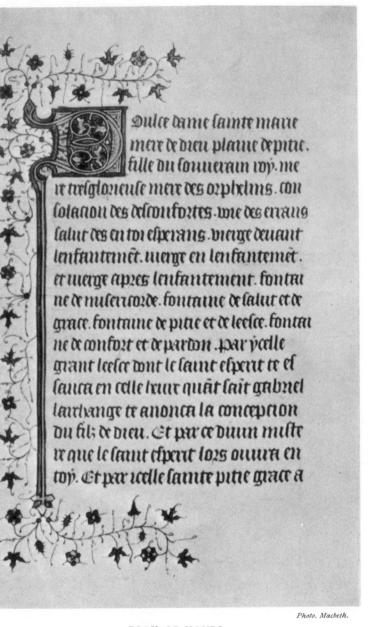

BOOK OF HOURS.

French, 14th Century, Brit. Mus.

To face page 176.

HARL. MS. 4425, BRIT. MUS.

blazing logs, the long days of winter were spent in chess-playing, broidery, lute-playing, and love-making, the monotony of this only occasionally broken by the arrival of some wandering minstrel who sang of war and love, or of some packman laden with sundry wares prized of womankind. But in winter such wayfarers were rare, and life was, perforce, one of boredom and discomfort. Thus there was exceeding joy when "woods and thickets donned their rich green mantling of resplendent sheen."

It is generally of springtime in a garden—a garden of green glades and alleys, fruit-trees and flowers, such as was very dear to the mediæval soul — of which we read. The *Roman de la Rose* opens with a description of a garden, hemmed round with castle wall—a pleasaunce within a fortress—and planted with trees "from out the land of Saracens," and many others, to wit, the pine, the beech (loved of squirrels), the graceful birch, the shimmering aspen, the hazel, the oak, and many flowers withal—roses and violets and periwinkle, golden king-cups, and pink-rimmed daisies. The poet describes with careful detail the design of the garden :

> The garden was nigh broad as wide,
> And every angle duly squared ;

how the trees were planted :

> Such skilful art
> Had planned the trees that each apart
> Six fathoms stood, yet like a net
> The interlacing branches met ;

and how "channelled brooks" flowed from clear fountains through "thymy herbage and gay flowers."

The debt which the mediæval world owed to the East is shown both in the fruits and the spices which are described as growing in the garden, and in the pastimes said to have been enjoyed in its cool shade. We read of pomegranates, nutmegs, almonds, dates, figs, liquorice, aniseed, cinnamon, and zedoary, an Eastern plant used as a stimulant. When the poet would tell of dance and song, he goes by

> A shaded pathway, where my feet,
> Bruised mint and fennel savouring sweet,

to a secluded lawn. Here he sees one whose name is " Gladness " :

> Gently swaying, rose and fell
> Her supple form, the while her feet
> Kept measured time with perfect beat :
>
> .   .   .   .   .
>
> While minstrels sang, the tambourine
> Kept with the flute due time I ween.
>
> .   .   .   .
>
> Then saw I cunning jugglers play,
> And girls cast tambourines away
> Aloft in air, then gaily trip
> Beneath them, and on finger-tip
> Catch them again.

In every garden there was a fountain or sheet of water with a small channelled way carrying the water to the castle and through the women's apartment. Sometimes these waterways were made use of by the lover as a means of communication with his beloved, as we read in the

romance of *Tristan and Isolde*, where Tristan,
to apprise his mistress that he is at their tryst-
ing-place in the garden, drops into the water
small pieces of bark and twigs, which are
quickly carried to the chamber where Isolde is
waiting and watching. And one eventide a
perilous encounter befalls. Tristan has been
banished the Court, for evil tongues have
whispered in King Mark's ear of his love for
Isolde, and have further whispered of secret
meetings in the garden, beside the fountain.
Now near the fountain is a pine-tree, into which
King Mark resolves to climb, and perchance to
discover the meeting of the lovers. As daylight
fades, Tristan scales the wall, and hastens to
throw into the water the little signals for his
lady. But as he stoops over the pool he sees,
reflected in its clear surface, the image of the
king, with bow ready bent. Can he stop the
floating twigs as they are hurried along on their
mission ? No. The water carries them away
out of sight, and Isolde must come. She comes,
but Tristan does not go to meet her as was his
wont, but remains standing by the water. She
wonders at her lover's seeming unconcern, but
as she approaches him, suddenly, in the bright
moonlight, she, too, sees in the water the
reflection of the king, and the lovers are saved.

A pine-tree is so often mentioned as a special
feature in a mediæval garden that one is led to
think that its use may either have been a survival
from the days of Tree Worship, seeing that the

tree was sacred to Adonis, Attis, and Osiris [1] (all, perhaps, varying forms of one and the same divinity), or have been suggested by some northern Saga. It makes its appearance in the *Chanson de Roland*, which has come down to us in a thirteenth-century form, incorporating the earlier Epic of *Roland*, probably composed towards the end of the eleventh century. In this we find mention of it when Charlemagne, after he is said to have taken Cordova, retires to a garden with Roland and Oliver and his barons, the elder ones amusing themselves with chess and tric-trac, and the younger ones with fencing, the king meanwhile looking on, seated under a pine-tree. Later in the day tents are set up, in which they pass the night, and in the early morning Charlemagne, after hearing mass, again sits under the pine-tree to take counsel of his barons.

In the *Roman de la Rose*, the fateful fountain of Narcissus is described as being beneath a pine-tree, which is represented as being taller and fairer than any that mortal eye had seen since the glorious pine of Charlemagne's time, showing that here at least the poet is making use of tradition.

But to make our way into a mediæval garden, and see all that grows therein, we must needs get within the precincts of the castle, for inside its fortified enclosure the castle, like a small village, was self-contained. And this was

[1] J. G. Frazer, *Adonis, Attis, Osiris*, 1906.

FLEMISH MASTER.

Fifteenth Century. Stephenson Clarke Collection.

To face page 181.

no easy matter, if we may judge from the vivid description to be found in *Huon de Bordeaux*, a poem concerning a Bordelais lord of the ninth century. After sundry adventures, Huon sets out on a journey to Babylon, and seeks an audience with the Emir. He tells of his arrival at what he describes as the castle, and how, after long parley with the porter, the drawbridge is let down and the great gate opened, and he finds himself in an arched way, with a series of portcullises showing their teeth overhead. After further parley, and further opening of gates, he enters a large courtyard, and goes thence into the garden, which is planted with every kind of tree, aromatic herb, and sweet-scented flower. In the garden is a fountain with its little channelled way, supplied with water from the Earthly Paradise. This description may seem a little fantastic, but it is only the poet's way of telling us what we might ourselves experience if we would go in imagination to some thirteenth- or fourteenth-century castle, and seek to gain admittance.

Sometimes the garden was within the castle fortifications. It was then necessarily circumscribed, and would, more or less, be laid out with formal pathways and stone-curbed borders, also with trees cut in various devices (a reminder of Rome's once far-reaching influence), and a tunnel or pergola of vines or sweet-scented creepers running the length of the wall to form a covered walk for shelter against sunshine or shower. But where the garden was without the fortifications, but yet within the castle enclosure, as was always the arrangement if possible, opportunity was afforded for wooded dell and flowery slope, as well as for the orchard with its special patch for herb-growing.

The herb-plot was one of the most important items in a mediæval garden ; for here were grown not only herbs and roots for healing, but also sweet-scented mint and thyme for mingling with the rushes strewn on the floors. Sometimes the rushes themselves were fragrant, and such, lemon-scented when crushed, may even to-day be found in the neighbourhood of Oxford, probably growing in the very place which at one time supplied many a college hall with its carpet of fresh green.

In the larger gardens might also be found labyrinths and aviaries, with bright-plumaged birds from the East. Here, too, were often enclosures for wild beasts, much prized by the lord of the castle, to whom they may have been proffered as peace-offerings, or as friendly gifts from some neighbouring lord. Strange beasts were royal gifts ; for kings, we read, made such offerings to each other. Even as early as the ninth century, Haroun al Raschid sent an elephant to Charlemagne. It was brought to Aix-la-Chapelle by Isaac the Jew, and survived its long walk seven years, and it would be interesting to know by what route it journeyed thither in those days. These private zoological

MS. ROMANCE OF ALEXANDER.
Fourteenth Century.

gardens may possibly account for the comparative accuracy with which the early miniaturists
painted such beasts as lions, bears, and leopards,
which otherwise they might have had no chance
of studying.

One of the greatest delights of the garden
was the bower in which the warm months were
passed. Here meals were taken, and merry
pastimes enjoyed, as long as daylight lasted.
Hither came tumblers and dancing-girls, and
sometimes performing animals. A poor captive
bear would be made to stumble over the rough
roads for miles in order to go through its
grotesque antics before some joyous company
of dames and gallants. But spring and youth
was the time to be gay, and nothing came amiss
to these light-hearted folk.

The bower was also the " privy playing
place," and all care was taken to make its leafy
screen grow close and thick. Perhaps one of
the most interesting references to a green arbour
—interesting because of the romance which was
the cause of its mention—is in a poem by King
James I. of Scotland, telling of sad years in prison,
which ended in love and liberty. James, whilst
still a young man, was imprisoned in Windsor
Castle, and writing to solace himself with something more tangible than the mere contemplation
of his beloved one, and to while away time,
describes the garden with " herbere green,"
which he saw through the barred window of
his prison-house. Leaning his head against the

cold stone wall, by night he gazed at the stars, by day at the garden. And weary and woe-begone as he was, he says, " to look, it did me good."

> Now there was made fast by the tower wall
> A garden fair, and in the corners set
> A herbere green, with wands so long and small
> Railed all about : and so with trees close set
> Was all the place, and hawthorn hedges knit
> That no one though he were near walking by
> Might there within scarce any one espy.

> So thick the branches and the leafage green
> Beshaded all the alleys that there were,
> And 'midst of ev'ry herbere might be seen
> The sharp and green sweet-scented juniper,
> Growing so fair with branches here and there,
> That, as it seemed to any one without,
> The branches spread the herbere all about.

> And on the slender green-leaved branches sat
> The little joyous nightingales, and sang
> So loud and clear, the carols consecrat
> To faithful love.[1]

This " garden fair " was the scene of the romance which solaced this royal prisoner, and helped him to bear his irksome lot, and to be able to exclaim, after nearly eighteen years' captivity— a captivity since boyhood :

> Thanks be to the massive castle wall,
> From which I eagerly looked forth and leant.

Looking from his window he espied, notwithstanding " hawthorne hedges " and " beshaded alleys," Lady Johanna Beaumont (whom he wedded on his release) walking in the garden. Neither poet nor historian tells how they found

---

[1] *King's Quair*, verse 31 *seq.*

RHENISH MASTER.

To face page 185.

means to communicate with one another, but tradition, which is sometimes twin-brother to truth, has handed down the story of a go-between who conveyed missives and tokens.

In the accompanying picture we see a corner of a mediæval garden, hemmed round with castle wall. In it the artist has adapted an everyday scene to a religious purpose, by giving my lady a crown, and the baby an aureole, to suggest the Holy Mother and Child, whilst one of the gentlemen-in-waiting is provided with wings, so as to make him more in harmony with such saintly company. But this is only what might have been seen on any bright morning in late spring or summer, in some castle pleasaunce. My lady reads a book, whilst her maidens amuse themselves, one holding a psaltery on which the child tinkles, to its evident delight and wonderment; another, with a perverted sporting instinct, seems to be trying to catch fish with a ladle (note the usual little channelled way, on which a bird is perched, refreshing itself), whilst a third is picking fruit. The three squires are doubtless talking of the chase, for, in my lady's presence, love would hardly be their theme. And all around are beautiful flowers—roses, lilies, and irises. Over against the enclosing wall is the usual bank of earth, faced with wood to keep it the necessary height, and planted with many flowers. This raised portion enabled those in the garden to get a view over the surrounding country, and to have a point of outlook in case of attack. It also served as a seat ; for at intervals, between the flowers and sweet-scented herbs, portions were covered with turf.

Of all the flowers in the garden the rose "red and pale" was the greatest favourite, and many different sorts were planted there. To so many purposes were they put, and so great was the demand for them, that large quantities of roses frequently served as the payment of vassals to their lord. They were used for strewing the floor at the wedding-feast, or at the entertaining of some great baron. The fresh petals were sprinkled over the surface of the water in the bath, and were distilled to make the rose-water with which the knights and ladies washed their hands and faces when they left their much-curtained beds. Further, they were specially prized for garlands, the making of which was one of the favourite occupations of the ladies of the Middle Ages. Dante, who sums up the spirit of the Middle Ages from the simplest reality to the sublimest ideal, alludes to garlands and garland-making as amongst the joys of the Earthly Paradise. In his poet's vision of the pageant of the Church Militant he sees the last company wreathed with red roses, emblems to him of Charity or Love. Boccaccio, in a more mundane atmosphere and a less august assemblage, also introduces us to this mediæval love of garlands. In a preamble to one of his tales he gives a dainty picture of the manners and pastimes of the gay folk of his day. Of the merry com-

HARL. MS. 4425, BRIT. MUS.

To face page 186.

pany, which his fancy makes to quit plague-
stricken Florence for the country, where they tell
stories to prevent monotony, he relates that, after
dining in the cool shade, and before the story-
telling begins, "the gentlemen walked with the
ladies into a goodly garden, making chaplets and
nosegays of divers flowers, and singing silently
to themselves." Both sexes wore them on festive
occasions, and in summer young girls wore no
head-covering save a garland. The knight at
the tournament decked his helm with a chaplet
of some chosen flower, deftly woven by the fair
one in whose name he made venture ; and many
a merry company, wreathed with flowers or
foliage, rode forth on May-day, with trumpets
and flutes, to celebrate the festival.

Another favourite flower for garlands was the
cornflower, as we learn from the poets, who tell
of ladies dancing the carole (a popular dance in
which all moved slowly round in a circle, singing
at the same time), their heads crowned with
garlands of cornflower. Violets and periwinkles,
and meadow flowers, white, red, and blue, were
also gathered to indulge this pretty fancy.

The gillyflower is another flower frequently
mentioned. This name has been applied to
various flowers, but originally it belonged to the
carnation, and was used for such in Shakespeare's
time. In the *Roman de la Rose* it is called the
gillyflower-clove, thus definitely defining it. One
of its virtues, according to an old writer, was
" to comfort the spirites by the sence of smelling,"

and also "to be of much use in ornament." But indeed most flowers were not only used for chaplets, and for strewing on the floor, but were also painted on the chamber walls, and embroidered on the hangings, to serve in winter days as sweet memories and as sweeter hopes.

Apparently the earliest records of gardens, after Roman times, date from the ninth century, and are mostly to be found amongst monastic archives. A garden was an important, and even essential, annex of a monastery, not only because of the "herbularis" or physic garden, from the herbs of which the monks compounded salves and potions for the wounded knight or the plundered wayfarer who might take shelter within its protecting walls, but also because of the solace which the shady trees and the gay flowers brought to the sick, for a monastery was generally a hospital as well. St. Bernard of Clairvaux, speaking of an abbey garden, gives a charming picture of one of these cloistered pleasaunces for the sick and the aged. He says :

Within the enclosure of this wall many and various trees, prolific in various fruits, constitute an orchard resembling a wood, which, being near the cell of the sick, lightens the infirmities of the brethren with no moderate solace, while it affords a spacious walking place to those who walk and a sweet place for reclining to those who are overheated. Where the orchard terminates the garden begins. Here also a beautiful spectacle is exhibited to the infirm brethren : while they sit upon the green margin of the huge basin, they see the little fishes playing under the water and representing a military encounter by swimming to meet each other.

MEDIÆVAL GARDENS

This warlike note seems strange and almost discordant in the midst of the peace of the cloister; but many, before seeking shelter there, had been doughty knights, and St. Bernard, man of the world as he was, would realise that even this mimic warfare might bring diversion to their tranquil seclusion.

What a contrast to all this joy in the Middle Ages in gardens and flowers are the sober reflections of Marcus Aurelius! Philosopher as he was, he would have us learn from plants the lesson of cause and effect, the continuity of life. He says :

> The destruction of one thing is the making of another ; and that which subsists at present is, as it were, the seed of succession, which springs from it. But if you take seed in the common notion, and confine it to the field or the garden, you have a dull fancy.

It is with a sense of relief that we turn from the thoughts which a garden suggests to this stoic, to those not less profound, though perhaps more simple, of a Chinese writer of the fourth century :

> Ah, how short a time it is that we are here! Why then not set our hearts at rest, ceasing to trouble whether we remain or go? What boots it to wear out the soul with anxious thoughts? Let me stroll through the bright hours as they pass in my garden among my flowers.

Printed by R. & R. CLARK, LIMITED, *Edinburgh.*